Contemporary
COOKING

Volume 8

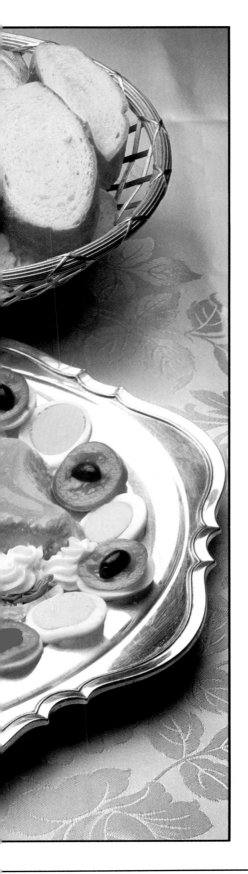

Contemporary
COOKING

Volume 8

3M

Contemporary Cooking

**Editorial production by James Charlton Associates, Ltd.,
New York. Editor-in-Chief, James Charlton; Executive Edi-
tor, Cara DeSilva; Managing Editors, Barbara Binswanger,
Jennie McGregor; Food Editors, Helen Feingold, Inez M.
Krech, Betsy Lawrence, Anne Lanigan, Maria Robbins,
Joan Whitman.**

**Book production and manufacturing consulting by:
Cobb/Dunlop Publishing Services, Inc., New York
Art Direction and interior design by:
Marsha Cohen/Parallelogram**

**Acknowledgments: Pat Cocklin, Delu PAL International,
Alan Duns, John Elliott, Gus Francisco Photography, Mel-
vin Grey, Gina Harris, Anthony Kay, Paul Kemp, David
Levin, David Meldrum, Roger Phillips, Nick Powell, Iain
Reid, John Turner, Paul Williams, George Wright, Cuisin-
arts, Inc.**

Printed and bound in Yugoslavia by CGP Delo.

Library of Congress Cataloging in Publication Data
Main entry under title:

Contemporary Cooking.

  Includes index.
  1. Cookery. I. Minnesota Mining and Manufacturing
Company.
TX715.C7586   1984   641.5   84-2563
0-88159-500-4 — (set)
ISBN: 0-88159–007–X

CONTENTS
for the Contemporary Cooking Series
VOLUME 8

Part One
SEAFOOD APPETIZERS

"Want some sea food, mama!
Shrimpers and rice, that's very nice!"

—Thomas ("Fats") Waller

The first food tasted in a meal dramatically sets the stage for all that follows and few other foods are so well suited to this place of honor on a menu as the delicacies that come to us from beneath the waters of the seas. Perhaps it is the clean fresh salty taste of seafood that makes it so stimulating to the palate, or perhaps it is merely that so many sea creatures are just naturally bite-size, but whatever the reason, shrimps, scallops, oysters and the like have done much of their considerable service to mankind as appetizers.

Perhaps also these dainty items are and have been increasingly more valued as delectable hors d'oeuvre than main course because their cost has escalated through the years.

The same can be said of caviar—the food of kings and king of all seafood appetizers.

"If it were not a pleasure, it would be an imperative duty to eat caviare.
. . . It is said that when sturgeon are in season, no less than two-thirds of the female consists of roe. It is certainly odd to think of a fish weighing perhaps 1,000 pounds being two-thirds made up of eggs.
. . . At such a rate of reproduction, the world would soon become the abode of sturgeons alone, were it not that the roe is exceedingly good."

(*Kettner's Book of the Table*, 1877)

"In this modern age when writing about caviar one has the feeling that it should be in the form of an obituary, as the world supply has dwindled to a trickle and its price has risen to such heights that it can no longer be classed as a mere fishery product."

(*The Encyclopedia of Fish Cookery*, 1977)

In the one hundred years that passed between the first astonishing statement and the second sad lament, the sturgeon (one of the world's oldest fish) nearly became extinct, a victim of overfishing and industrial pollution.

Although the finest caviar has always come from the sturgeon of the Caspian Sea (the world's largest salt water lake), the Black Sea and the Sea of Azov, sturgeon were once so plentiful in the United States that caviar was given away in the late 1800s at the free-lunch counters of the big saloons with the purchase of a nickel beer. The population of sturgeon in the Hudson River was, in fact, so huge that it was dubbed "Albany beef" and sold for only pennies a pound. Until Henry Schacht established his caviar business on the Delaware River in 1873, the roes of these huge 200-pound fish were considered worthless. Then for a brief and profitable time the Delaware River fishery was producing vast quantities of caviar—anywhere from 270 to 600 *tons* per year. Much of this caviar was exported to countries all over the world and much of it was re-imported by unscrupulous merchants and passed off as "Russian" caviar at many times the original price. But by 1900, only 27 years later, the American caviar industry was dead. The once abundant sturgeon had been fished out. On the West Coast a similar story repeated itself.

In Russia, caviar (*ikra*) has been made since the thirteenth century. It was known in early Persia as *chavjar,* literally the "food of strength," because it was believed to have great healing powers as well as properties that endowed potency. But whether it was for the taste or for the stimulating side effects, the finest caviar and the greatest quantity of it has always been reserved for royalty. Tsar Nicholas II levied a tax on sturgeon fishers, which brought approximately eleven tons of top-grade caviar to the royal tables every year, including almost the entire yield of the rarest of all caviars, the golden roe of sterlet, a small variety of sturgeon found only in the rivers of the Caspian. Stalin apparently continued this distinctly un-proletarian tradition and yearly reserved a vast portion of the finest caviar for his own use, as did the Shah of Iran. Today, alas, even the Caspian Sea is choked with industrial pollution so that both in Russia and Iran the sturgeon population is only a fraction of what it once was.

Despite astonishing prices, caviar remains the most sought-after of all seafood appetizers, and its appearance on a dinner table anywhere in the world is an extravagant gesture of hospitality. Fortunately for those of us whose tastes exceed our pocketbooks, there are a great many other prepared roes that in their own way make as dramatic and delicious a beginning course.

Many varieties of smoked fish also fall into the luxury class of foods that make for lavish openings to important meals. Originally smoking was used chiefly for its preservative effect so that the fish that were caught in times of abundance might last through the more meager days of winter. Today, however, the smoking process is employed primarily for the fine and unique texture and taste that it imparts.

Of course, seafood need not be astronomically expensive even as an appetizer. Shrimp, crab meat and lobster can be within reach especially when combined and stretched in salads, mousses and spreads. In season, scallops, clams, mussels and even oysters can be elegant yet inexpensive beginnings to a meal.

SEAFOOD APPETIZERS

Nothing beats an appetizer of seafood when you want to give a meal a distinctive air of opulence. Smoked salmon, osietr caviar, and lobster are the epitome of luxury to many, and are usually reserved for special occasions. However, smoked trout, pressed caviar and shrimps are also admirable, as are the delicious clam, crab, oyster and fish dishes presented in this chapter, especially the elegant mousses and other classic appetizers.

The simplest preparations are often the best. Favorites with all seafood fanciers are clams on the half-shell and oysters on the half-shell; steamed softshell clams and steamed mussels are also popular; see Volume 7 Index for all of these. Seafood salads, made of freshly cooked fish or shellfish, or mixtures of two or more kinds, are simple to prepare and delicious. Mix the seafood with Mayonnaise, Rémoulade Sauce or Aïoli (see Volume 3 Index for sauces) and pile on a bed of shredded lettuce or in a single perfect lettuce leaf. The salad can be augmented with chopped green or red bell pepper, cucumber, celery, scallion, etc., and a final sprinkling of chopped parsley or chives adds an attractive finish. Shrimp Cocktail (see Volume 3 Index) is an international favorite in demand everywhere; crab meat can be served in the same fashion.

Hot seafood appetizers, such as small portions of Seafood Quiche (see Volume 2 Index), are also delicious. Try broiled shad roe or other roes on toast, or small portions of any freshly cooked fish topped with a spoonful of hollandaise or curry sauce, garnished with cucumber balls.

Luxurious Roes

Hard roe is the egg sac of the female fish and is made up of numerous tiny eggs. Soft roe, known as milt, comes from the male fish. Roe is always impressive as an appetizer, whether it is the expensive caviar or the more modest cod roe, which can be used in a number of ways.

Caviar. The only true caviar is the hard roe of a sturgeon. Large sturgeons, from which the best caviar comes, are now found only in the Caspian Sea so quality caviar is almost exclusively a Russian and Iranian product; consequently, it is rare and extremely expensive. Though American sturgeons are not the large variety, domestic caviar, increasingly available, has improved in quality and is less costly.

To enjoy it at its best you need to eat caviar as fresh as possible. Needless to say, most people have to be content with the slightly muted flavor of pasteurized caviar from jars and cans that can be bought in specialty food stores.

The three kinds of true caviar are named after the species of sturgeon that supplies the roe—beluga, osietr and sevruga.

Beluga comes from the largest fish, between 16 and 20 years old, and is the most expensive. Color varies from pale gray to pitch black and the grains are large.

Osietr comes from slightly smaller fish and is the rarest. It has a stronger flavor than beluga. The color can vary from golden brown through to gray, green and black.

Sevruga comes from smaller fish, 7 to 10 years old, and the grains are therefore smaller too. It has a superb flavor, is the most readily available, and is also the cheapest of the real caviars.

Pausnaya or pressed caviar. This is made from leftover roes of various species of sturgeon and pressed into barrels. The flavor is good. It is much less expensive than fresh caviar and is widely used by caterers for fillings and garnishes.

Malosol means lightly salted. All kinds of roe can be prepared with little salt, and are considered to be fresh, whereas pressed caviar is often more heavily salted, which makes it less delicate than the other types.

Mock caviar comes from the roe of fish such as cod and salmon, rather than sturgeon.

Red caviar comes from salmon and it is greatly appreciated for its beautiful golden-red color. Its taste is unlike true caviar but it has a good flavor of its own. It makes stylish cocktail snacks or a tasty filling with sour cream for blini (small buckwheat pancakes).

Lumpfish caviar is a black- or red-dyed mock caviar produced from the roe of the lumpfish. Although it is nothing like real caviar in flavor, it makes a dramatic garnish for smoked salmon canapés, open sandwiches and cold savory mousses. It is widely available in small jars at relatively modest cost.

Serving caviar. Once bought, the important thing is to keep fresh, pasteurized or mock caviar chilled but not frozen. Keep it just below the frozen food compartment in a refrigerator and eat it within a day or two.

Although caviar is frequently served with accompaniments, its fine flavor is best appreciated unadorned, accompanied by nothing except a dry cracker or freshly made thin toast. Send it to the table in its container, surrounded with ice cubes. For an average portion allow 1 to 1½ ounces. Pressed caviar can be served on small dry crackers as cocktail snacks.

Preserved Fish

Fish loses its freshness very quickly and can be dangerous if eaten when stale. The eating period can be extended if fish is treated immediately after it is caught. Preservation methods include salting, pickling, smoking, drying, freezing and canning.

The oldest method is brining (immersing fish in heavily salted water) and this process is still used today to tenderize, flavor and preserve fish. Oily fish need more than brine to preserve them if they are to be kept for any length of time, so they are smoked afterward, which also flavors the fish and gives it such a delicious piquant taste that even nonoily fish, which do not need the additional preservative, are often smoked simply for the flavor.

Smoked fish, be it expensive salmon from the northern seas, delicate smoked river trout or more mundane smoked mackerel or porgy, make delicious and easy appetizers. They can be served all on their own, with just a wedge of juicy lemon or with a tangy sharply flavored sauce. Although the principles of different types of curing and smoking are basically similar, the same species of fish tastes different when bought from different smokers. So shop around to find the cure most to your liking.

There are two main methods of smoking fish—at a high or relatively low temperature.

Hot-smoked fish. After brining, the fish is smoked in a kiln with the temperature raised to a degree high enough to cook the fish right through. Fish smoked in this way—trout, chubs (whitefish) and eel, for example—can be served without further cooking. All are usually available from delicatessens and fish markets.

Cold-smoked fish. After brining, the fish is smoked at a relatively

Dressing a Crab

1 Lay crab on its back with tail flap toward you. Twist off legs and claws close to the body.

2 Press upward from beneath tail flap and force shell and body apart with fingers or tip of a knife.

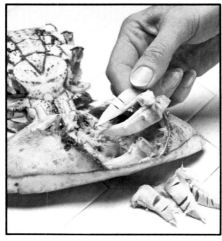

3 Remove and discard the gills from the body section of the crab.

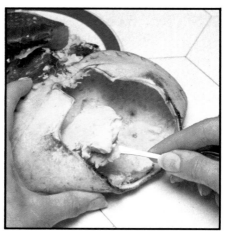

7 In some crabs a curdish type of meat is found close to the shell. Scrape it into the bowl.

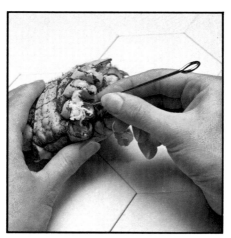

8 Dig meat out of hollows left by legs and claws and from the center with a skewer.

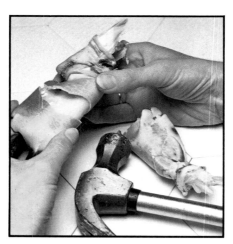

9 Crack large claws and remove white meat and pinkish curd.

low temperature. Most fish prepared in this way—including haddock, kipper, whiting and fillets of cod—need to be lightly cooked before eating. Inevitably there are exceptions to these rules. Smoked salmon, which is cold smoked, is nearly always served without further cooking.

Choosing and storing smoked fish. The flavor of smoked fish is best when freshly cured, so when buying always look for signs of freshness. These are firm flesh, glossy skin and a wholesome fresh smoked smell. Avoid tired-looking fish that has shriveled and looks dried.

Before the days of refrigeration, heavy salting and prolonged smoking were necessary to preserve fish. Nowadays brining and smoking are light, as they are intended mainly as a means of flavoring fish. The preservative effect is slight. Therefore smoked fish should be refrigerated and kept for not much longer than the fresh equivalent.

Serving smoked fish. The classic way to serve smoked fish is simple: with wedges of juicy lemon to flavor it and dark bread and butter as an accompaniment. This is not only a treat for diners but a delight for the cook since so little work is involved. Diners can either skin and fillet the fish

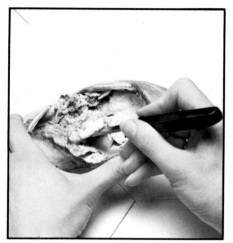

4 Remove and discard the green-brown stomach sac, which lies just below the head.

5 The firm meat is left with no remains of the gills or stomach.

6 Carefully scrape meat from shell into a bowl, using handle of teaspoon to reach under shell.

10 Crack legs to extract the small amount of meat, or leave whole for garnishing.

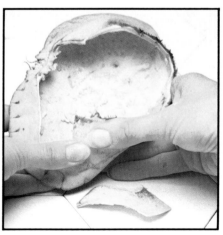

11 To use the shell for serving, tap gently along the inside of the natural line mark and break it away.

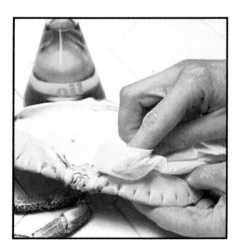

12 Scrub shell, inside and out, dry, and rub with oil to make it shine. Oil any legs for garnishing.

Filleting Smoked Trout

1 Cut off the tail; if the head is present, remove that too.

2 Cut through the skin along the length of the back.

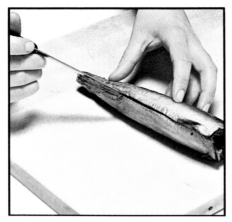

3 Cut through the skin from the end of belly cavity to the tail.

4 Lift skin with the tip of a knife and peel it back.

5 Carefully turn the fish over. Peel skin off the other side.

6 Cut through the flesh from the belly cavity to the tail end.

7 Gently ease the fish open to lie flat, exposing the backbone.

8 Starting at the head end, lift out the backbone.

9 Scrape away the dark skin of the belly cavity and remaining bones.

themselves or this can be done in advance, a very easy procedure (see Filleting Smoked Trout). Salmon is often served with a little pile of minced onion and a heap of capers.

For the richer, oilier smoked fish, such as sturgeon and sable, it is a good idea to serve an accompanying sharply flavored sauce, either as a substitute for or in addition to wedges of lemon. Two delicious cold sauces are given in the recipe section.

Some smoked fish can be marinated to make delicious salads, and various types make excellent bases for pâtés, creams and mousses. These are all popular first courses and are equally useful for buffet parties and to accompany drinks, topping cocktail canapés, filling miniature pastry cases, stuffing celery and so on.

The richest pâtés are simply made from skinned and filleted fish pounded with unsalted butter and seasoning. Lighter textured, less rich mixtures can be made by replacing some of the butter with cream, cream cheese, cottage cheese, hard-cooked egg, or even a small proportion of fresh bread crumbs, which also makes the pâté go a little further.

Fish and Shellfish Mousses

Deceptively easy to make, creamy savory mousses are just the thing when you want to impress without making too much of an effort and spending hours in the kitchen.

A smooth amalgamation of fish, crabs or shrimps with cream, cream cheese or yogurt, or a rich white sauce, these mousses are set with gelatin and chilled until firm. Made in a pretty mold and garnished tastefully, they make an attractive center point for a meal and, because they are set, can be made well in advance, saving precious time. Actual cooking time is very short. The only slightly complicated aspect is the handling of gelatin, and once you get this right, the art of mousse-making will be yours.

Ingredients. Savory mousses are made of flavoring, binding or liquid,

gelatin and sometimes a lightening of whipped cream or beaten egg white.

Fish. Both fresh and smoked, fish is excellent for mousses. It should be flaked, pounded or puréed. Smoked salmon, haddock, mackerel and trout are very good. Canned fish, especially tuna and salmon, also make good quick mousses.

Shellfish. Crab, lobster and shrimps make delicious but rather expensive mousses. The flesh of these shellfish should be pounded in a mortar with a pestle or puréed in a food processor.

Bindings. To hold the mousse together and to give a liquid element for the gelatin to act on and make a smooth jelly, a binding is used. This can be either white sauce, which is usually enriched by beating in 2 egg yolks after the sauce has been made, or mayonnaise.

If the flavoring is quite thick—like cream cheese or avocado purée—canned consommé or stock may be used. Cream—both light and heavy—is sometimes used to enrich the mousse and usually mixed with another binding. Both light and heavy cream are used, depending on the other ingredients. Mayonnaise, plain yogurt, sour cream, and white sauce are used with many fish mousses, as are cream cheese and cottage cheese.

Gelatin. Powdered gelatin is sold in small envelopes each weighing ¼ ounce (7 grams), about 1 tablespoon. There are usually several packets to a box. Follow manufacturer's instructions carefully for softening and dissolving the gelatin.

Gelatin is never added to a mixture in its dry state but is always dissolved in liquid. Correct dissolving is very important to the quality of the dish being made. First soften the gelatin in cold liquid. This can be water or part of the liquid used in the recipe. Generally 1 packet of gelatin is softened in 4 tablespoons liquid, but follow recipe instructions carefully, as the amount of liquid will have been carefully worked out in proportion to the other ingredients.

Sprinkle the powder in the liquid

in a heavy pan. Leave for about 5 minutes. The gelatin will become slightly translucent as it absorbs the liquid.

To melt the gelatin so that it can be mixed easily with other ingredients, it is placed over heat. The heat must be very low; otherwise the gelatin will thicken and be useless. If necessary, use a heat diffuser or an asbestos mat underneath the pan. Warm the liquid gently until it is clear. On no account allow it to boil. Do not stir; this causes the gelatin to wash against the sides of the pan and stick to it, which means a loss of some gelatin and an alteration of the balance of the ingredients, so you don't have quite the right amount of gelatin needed for setting.

When the gelatin has been dissolved, it must be used immediately. This is especially important when adding it to a cold liquid, otherwise it may set in threads before the mixing is finished.

Adding the gelatin and combining ingredients. Gelatin is always added to the base in a thin stream. The mixture is stirred all the time the gelatin is being added. This insures thorough mixing and prevents the gelatin setting in threads. To avoid waste, scrape the gelatin out of the pan with a rubber spatula. Once the gelatin has been incorporated, the mixture is left to cool until it is on the point of setting. Stir the mixture from time to time during this period.

In some recipes, especially those where gelatin is combined with a hot mixture, you may find that the second melting stage has been omitted. The gelatin is softened initially in a larger amount of liquid than usual and then beaten into the prepared hot liquid for the mousse. Always follow recipe instructions carefully when doing this.

The only exception to the rule that the gelatin is added to the mousse base while it is still hot is when the base is a milk mixture. The gelatin must be left until lukewarm, otherwise the milk mixture may curdle.

Molding. First make sure that the mold is perfectly clean. If it isn't, the mousse may refuse to come out. To prevent sticking (a good idea even with

Salmon Mousse

12 portions

15 ounces canned salmon
2 cups milk, approximately
2 tablespoons butter
3 tablespoons all-purpose flour
1 envelope (1 tablespoon) unflavored gelatin
2 large eggs
½ cup light cream
1 tablespoon lemon juice
salt and black pepper
2 hard-cooked eggs
1 bunch of watercress paprika

1 Drain the liquid from the salmon into a 2-cup measure and add enough milk to fill cup.

2 Turn salmon into a large bowl. Remove any bones or skin and mash salmon with a large kitchen fork.

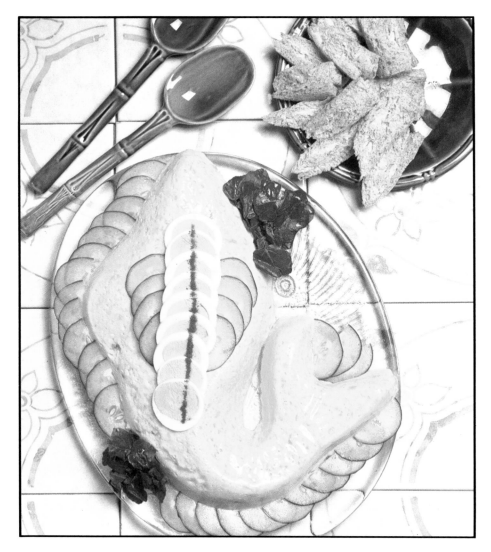

6 Set pan over low heat until gelatin is melted, about 3 minutes. Remove pan from heat.

10 Fold the cold fish mixture, 1 tablespoon at a time, into the beaten egg whites.

3 Melt the butter in a heavy pan over low heat. Remove from heat, stir in flour, then cook for 2 to 3 minutes.

4 Remove from heat; slowly stir in the milk. Return to heat. Bring to a boil, stirring. Reduce heat; cook for 10 minutes.

5 Pour ¼ cup cold water into a saucepan. Sprinkle the gelatin over the water and soak for 5 minutes.

7 Remove sauce from heat. Pour in the gelatin in a thin stream, stirring all the time.

8 Separate eggs and stir yolks into the sauce. Cool for 5 minutes. Stir in cream, mashed salmon and lemon juice. Season.

9 Place mixture in refrigerator until just setting. Beat egg whites until they stand in soft peaks.

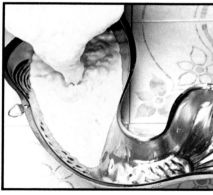

11 Rinse a 4-cup mold in cold water. Turn fish mixture into mold. Level top with a rubber-bladed spatula.

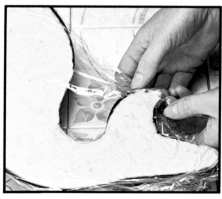

12 Cover mold and chill in refrigerator for 1½ hours. Unmold 30 minutes before you plan to serve it.

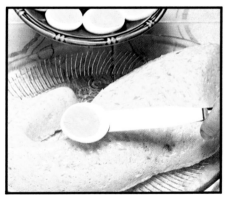

13 Peel and slice the hard-cooked eggs and arrange on the fish. Garnish with watercress. Sprinkle with paprika.

Taramasalata

Tarama is a paste made from carp roe. It can be found fresh or in the jar in Greek and Middle Eastern food stores, and is also sometimes sold in specialty food stores. Codfish roe is a less costly and more available substitute.

6 portions

5 ounces tarama, or 5 ounces cod roe, fresh
1 thick slice of white bread
1 garlic clove

1 cup olive oil
   freshly ground black pepper
2 tablespoons lemon juice
   black olives
   lemon wedges

1 If using fresh roe, place in a bowl. Pour on boiling water to cover completely. Leave for 1 minute.

4 Gently squeeze bread with your fingers to remove excess liquid, leaving a soft white pulp.

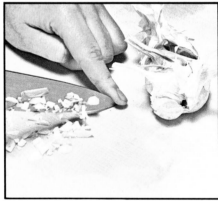

5 Using a sharp knife, peel the garlic and mince it.

6 Add the garlic, 2 tablespoons oil and some pepper to the bread and blend.

7 Add a walnut-size piece of roe, or several tablespoons of tarama, and some more oil. Blend until smooth.

8 Continue blending, adding a little roe or tarama and oil at a time, until a thick smooth paste is formed.

9 Blend in the lemon juice. Correct seasoning if necessary. Cover and refrigerate until required.

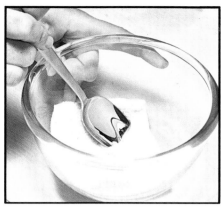

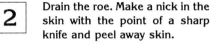

2 Drain the roe. Make a nick in the skin with the point of a sharp knife and peel away skin.

3 Cut crust from bread and pour on ¼ cup cold water. Press with a spoon until bread is mushy.

10 Transfer to a serving dish and garnish with black olives and lemon wedges. Serve with triangles of pita bread.

nonstick molds), rinse the mold with cold water.

The mold must be very cold before the mousse mixture is poured in. A good way to insure this is to place the mold in a freezer for a few minutes before pouring in the mixture. This cuts down the setting time of the mixture and, more important, helps the setting to start quickly.

Pour the mixture into the upside-down mold, scraping the bowl with a rubber spatula to get all of the mixture. Level the mixture in the mold with a rubber spatula. Cover with a plate or plastic wrap to prevent the mold from absorbing other food flavors from the refrigerator and place it, still upside down, on the coldest shelf of the refrigerator. Leave until firm, or for the time stated in the recipe.

Unmolding. This is the "moment of truth" that worries many mousse makers, but if you follow these instructions carefully, nothing should go wrong.

Have ready a sink or bowl full of very hot water. Select the dish on which you plan to stand the mousse. It should be flat and big enough to accommodate the mousse easily.

Uncover the mold and dip it into hot water. If using a metal mold, count to three. If using a porcelain or plastic mold, immerse for 5 seconds, as these molds are not good conductors of heat. Remove from the water and gently run a knife around the outer edge of the mold between mold and mousse. Invert the serving dish over the mold, then, holding dish and mold firmly together, turn over so the mold is the right way up.

Give the mold a sharp jerk. You will hear a sucking sound that shows the suction has been released. Gently lift the mold away from the mousse. If there is any extra liquid on the plate, mop it up with a paper towel. If the outer surface of the mousse has melted slightly because of the hot water, return it to the refrigerator for a few minutes to become firm.

It is best to unmold the mousse about 30 minutes before you are ready to serve it to allow the texture to soften slightly and the flavors to develop.

12

Crab in Shells

4 portions

1 cooked Dungeness crab, 2
    pounds, or 4 smaller crabs
2 tablespoons fresh bread
    crumbs
2 teaspoons lemon juice
    salt and pepper
1 tablespoon mayonnaise
1 hard-cooked egg
2 teaspoons minced fresh
    parsley
    paprika, or strips of red
    pimiento
    lettuce leaves
    sliced hard-cooked egg

1 Place half of crab meat in a bowl and add bread crumbs, 1 teaspoon lemon juice, and seasoning to taste.

2 Pack this mixture into the center of the shell, leaving room for remaining crab meat on either side.

3 Add 1 teaspoon lemon juice, the mayonnaise, and seasoning to taste to remaining crab meat.

4 Pile this mixture into the shell on both sides, keeping neat divisions between the 2 mixtures.

5 Mince the egg white and sieve the yolk and use to make dividing lines between the 2 mixtures.

6 Sprinkle egg and parsley in straight rows, keeping the lines close together but separate.

7 The yolk should be close to outer division, then the parsley, then egg white next to inner crab mixture.

8 Sprinkle thin diagonal lines of paprika in a diamond pattern across the outer portions.

9 Alternatively, lay thin strips of red pimiento in a diagonal pattern.

10 Surround crab with a few small legs, lettuce leaves and sliced hard-cooked egg, topped with pimiento, if used.

11 Serve with a crisp salad and whole-wheat bread and butter, or crusty tiny whole-wheat rolls and butter.

Horseradish Cream

1 cup

2 ounces fresh horseradish, or
   2 tablespoons prepared
   horseradish
½ cup heavy cream

2 tablespoons milk
1 teaspoon lemon juice
½ teaspoon sugar
   salt

Peel the fresh horseradish root and grate enough of it to make 2 tablespoons. If you are using prepared horseradish, drain it. Pour the cream and milk into a bowl and whisk or beat with a rotary beater until thick but not stiff. Stir in the lemon juice, horseradish, sugar, and salt to taste. Serve lightly chilled, as an accompaniment to smoked fish.

Variation: For mustard cream, substitute 1 tablespoon dry mustard for the horseradish.

Watercress and Walnut Sauce

1 cup

¼ cup shelled walnuts
1 bunch of watercress

½ cup dairy sour cream
   salt and pepper

Grind or chop the walnuts in a food processor or blender until reduced to fine crumbs. Wash the watercress and pull all the leaves off the stems. Reserve stems for stock or soup. Put the leaves in a large strainer and plunge it into boiling water for 1 minute. Lift out the strainer and plunge at once into cold water, then lift out and let the leaves drain. Press to extract all the water, then chop the watercress by hand or in a food processor or blender.

Turn the sour cream into a mixing bowl and stir until smooth. Add the walnuts and watercress and mix well. Season with salt and black pepper to taste. Serve with smoked fish.

Smoked Trout Pâté

6 portions

2 smoked trout, each 6 to 7
   ounces
½ cup sour cream
1 teaspoon prepared
   horseradish
1 teaspoon lemon juice

1 tablespoon chopped fresh
   parsley
4 ounces cream cheese
2 tablespoons butter, at room
   temperature
   black pepper

Cut off heads and tails from the trout, split them lengthwise and peel off the skin, then lift out the bones, taking care to remove all the small bones (see Index). Put the trout into a blender, or in a food processor fitted with the steel blade. Add the sour cream, horseradish, lemon juice and parsley, and blend or process until smooth. Add the cream cheese, butter, and pepper to taste, and blend or process again until smooth.

Check the seasoning; add more if needed. Turn the mixture into a 2- to 3-cup bowl and serve as part of a buffet bowl, or into six ⅓-cup pottery pots or custard cups and serve as an individual appetizer; pack the mixture firmly and smooth the top with a spatula. Cover and refrigerate until ready to use. Serve in the containers, with fresh toast or unsalted crackers.

Fisherman's Lemons

6 portions

6 large round lettuce leaves
6 large lemons
7½ ounces canned salmon or tuna
2 hard-cooked eggs
¼ teaspoon salt

¼ teaspoon black pepper
2 to 3 tablespoons mayonnaise or sour cream
1 tablespoon chopped fresh parsley

Line 6 flat serving dishes with the whole lettuce leaves. Halve the lemons and squeeze out all the juice; reserve 2 teaspoons of the juice. Scrape out and discard all membranes and remaining pulp in the lemon halves. Cut a slice off the bottom of each lemon half so that it has a flat base. Place 2 halves on each lettuce-lined dish.

Drain the canned fish and turn it into a mixing bowl.

Mash the fish with a fork. Peel and chop the eggs. Add the salt, pepper, mayonnaise or sour cream, reserved lemon juice and half of the chopped egg to the fish. Mix together well. Pile the mixture into the lemon halves. Sprinkle remaining chopped egg and the parsley on top. Place the dishes in the refrigerator and chill for at least 1 hour before serving.

Broiled Shrimps

6 to 8 portions

2 pounds large shrimps, fresh
  or frozen
1 garlic clove
4 tablespoons white wine
4 tablespoons olive oil
2 tablespoons tomato purée

2 teaspoons dried marjoram
1 tablespoon snipped fresh
  chives
1 teaspoon salt
¼ teaspoon black pepper

If the shrimps are fresh, shell and devein them. If they are frozen, place them in a shallow dish at room temperature and leave them to thaw for 1 hour; then drain and pat dry on paper towels.

Peel garlic and put through a press into a large bowl. Add remaining ingredients for the sauce. Add the shrimps and stir gently to coat them with the liquid. Marinate shrimps in a cool place for 4 hours.

When ready to cook, preheat the broiler. Pour the shrimps and the sauce into a shallow baking pan. Spread out the shrimps to make a single layer. Place the pan under the broiler about 5 inches from the heat source. Broil for about 3 minutes, basting frequently with the sauce in the pan. Turn shrimps over, baste again, and cook for 2 minutes longer, until they are pink and lightly browned on the edges.

With a slotted spoon remove the shrimps from the pan to a heated serving dish. Spoon a little of the sauce over the top. Strain remaining sauce into a sauceboat.

Potted Shrimps

3 or 4 portions

8 ounces cleaned cooked
  shrimps, weighed after
  peeling
2 tablespoons olive oil
½ teaspoon minced fresh basil

pinch of cayenne pepper
juice of 1 lime or ½ lemon
¼ teaspoon crushed coriander
  or cuminseed (optional)

Put the shrimps into the container of a blender or food processor and reduce to a paste. Gradually add the olive oil while processing the shrimps. Add basil, cayenne pepper, and the strained lime or lemon juice. Process again. When the mixture is smooth, add the spice if you use it, and check the seasoning. Salt may or may not be necessary, depending on how much has been used in poaching the shrimps.

Pack the paste in a little jar or terrine. Cover and store in the refrigerator for up to 2 days. Serve chilled, with toast.

Potted Crab

3 or 4 portions

8 ounces cooked crab meat,
  fresh, pasteurized or frozen
4 tablespoons butter
  salt, black pepper and
  cayenne pepper

2 teaspoons lemon juice
4 tablespoons clarified butter
  (see Volume 5 Index)

Pick over the crab meat to remove any bits of shell or cartilage. Pound crab until smooth. Melt the butter in a saucepan and add the seasonings to taste; add only a small shake of cayenne. Remove pan from heat and stir in the crab meat and the lemon juice. Pack the mixture into small pots or ramekins, about ½-cup size. Melt the clarified butter and pour a thin layer over the top of each pot to act as a seal and keep the crab fresh and moist. Let the pots cool and the butter become firm. Cover with plastic wrap and store in the refrigerator for up to 2 days.

Serve the potted crab sprinkled with minced fresh parsley and accompanied with crustless triangles of dark bread or hot thin toast.

Oysters Rockefeller

6 portions

8 ounces fresh spinach	¼ teaspoon black pepper
4 scallions	¼ teaspoon cayenne pepper
2 celery ribs	¼ cup light cream
3 parsley sprigs	3 tablespoons Pernod or other
rock salt	anise-flavored liqueur
1 teaspoon salt	36 fresh oysters, in the shell

Wash spinach thoroughly; remove any damaged leaves and all coarse stems. Place in a large saucepan and pour in enough boiling water to cover the spinach. Let stand for 1 minute, then drain the spinach in a colander, pressing it to extract as much water as possible. Wash and trim scallions and cut into short lengths. Wash and dry celery, trim it, and cut into short lengths. Wash and dry parsley and cut stems and leaves into small pieces.

Preheat oven to 450°F. Cover the bottom of 2 large baking pans with enough rock salt to make a layer ½ inch thick.

Place the spinach, scallions, celery, parsley, salt, black pepper, cayenne and cream in the container of an electric blender or food processor and blend or process, on and off, for 1 minute in the blender, or about 10 seconds in the processor, until all the ingredients are puréed. Transfer the purée to a mixing bowl. Pour in the Pernod and mix well.

Remove the top shell from each oyster and press the bottom shells into the rock salt until they are firm and level. Place half of the oysters in each baking pan. Cover each oyster with about 1 teaspoon of the vegetable purée. Set the pans in the oven and bake for 4 minutes. Remove pans from the oven. Use tongs or potholders to transfer the oysters to 6 individual serving dishes and serve immediately.

Marinated Oysters

4 portions

1	garlic clove
¾	cup dry white wine
¼	cup olive oil
¼	cup lemon juice
¼	teaspoon salt
¼	teaspoon black pepper
¼	teaspoon dried thyme
¼	teaspoon dried chervil
1	teaspoon minced fresh parsley
16	fresh oysters

Peel and crush the garlic and place in a glass or pottery bowl. Add all other ingredients except oysters and stir with a fork to mix well. Shuck the oysters and place them in a stainless-steel saucepan. Discard the shells. Add the marinade to the oysters and set the pan over moderate heat. Bring the liquid to a boil, then remove pan from heat. Transfer oysters and liquid to a serving bowl and set aside to cool to room temperature.

Serve the oysters cold, in their marinade.

Smoked Fish Appetizer

6 portions

4 ounces smoked salmon
1 small smoked trout, about 6 ounces
1 small smoked mackerel, 6 to 8 ounces
3 Marinated Kipper Fillets (see Index)
6 lemon wedges
6 seedless orange wedges
12 small gherkins
12 watercress sprigs

Cut salmon into thin slices and divide into 6 portions. Form the slices into rolls. Skin and fillet the trout and cut each fillet into 3 portions. Skin and fillet the mackerel and cut into small pieces of rough shape. Drain the kipper fillets from the marinade and cut each across into strips about ½ inch wide. Use scissors to do this as it is easier than using a knife.

Arrange a portion of each type of fish on 6 plates. Garnish each one with a lemon and an orange wedge, 2 gherkins and 2 watercress sprigs.

Deviled Crab on Toast

4 portions

1 small onion
2 tablespoons butter
½ cup fresh bread crumbs
1 teaspoon tomato paste
2 teaspoons minced chutney
few drops of Worcestershire sauce
1 tablespoon prepared mustard
4 drops of Tabasco®
salt and pepper
8 ounces cooked crab meat, fresh, pasteurized or frozen
4 to 8 slices of firm bread
minced parsley
lemon slices

Peel and mince the onion and sauté it gently in 1 tablespoon of the butter until soft but not browned. Add the bread crumbs, tomato purée, chutney, Worcestershire, mustard, Tabasco, and salt and pepper to taste. Pick over the crab meat to remove any bits of shell or cartilage. Add crab to the crumb mixture and stir gently. Heat well.

Toast the bread, butter it with remaining butter, and remove crusts. Spread the crab-meat mixture on the toasts and cut them into neat triangles or fingers. Garnish the toasts with minced parsley and a slice of lemon.

Avocado Stuffed with Crab

4 portions

2 avocados
1 tablespoon lemon juice
¼ cup shelled walnuts
6 to 8 ounces cooked crab meat, fresh, pasteurized or frozen
1 tablespoon olive oil
2 tablespoons wine vinegar
salt and black pepper
1 hard-cooked egg
2 teaspoons minced parsley

Halve the avocados lengthwise. Scoop out the flesh without damaging the skins; reserve the skins. Mash the avocado flesh with a fork or in a food processor or blender. Add the lemon juice to prevent discoloration. Chop the walnuts. Pick over the crab meat to remove any bits of shell or cartilage. Combine crab meat, walnuts, oil and vinegar, and season to taste. Add the mixture to the mashed avocado and mix gently. Spoon the mixture into the avocado shells, filling them to the top; smooth the top with a butter spreader.

Sieve the egg yolk and chop the white. Sprinkle sieved egg yolk and chopped egg white and the minced parsley over the stuffed avocados. Serve at once.

Crab au Gratin

6 portions

1 medium-size onion
2 celery ribs
2 tablespoons butter
4 ounces button mushrooms
1 cup Béchamel Sauce (see Volume 3 Index)
10 ounces cooked crab meat, fresh, pasteurized or frozen
1 tablespoon heavy cream

few drops of Worcestershire sauce
salt and pepper
2 ounces Parmesan cheese, grated (½ cup)
½ cup fresh white bread crumbs
parsley sprigs
few small shrimps for garnishing (optional)

Peel and mince the onion. Wash and dry the celery and cut into thin slices. Cook both in the butter over low heat until the onion is translucent and the celery softened. Wipe mushrooms with a damp cloth, trim base of stems, and cut caps and stems into thin slices. Add mushrooms to the pan and cook for 1 minute. Add the vegetables and any remaining butter to the béchamel sauce in a saucepan, then stir in the crab meat. Heat thoroughly, turning the mixture in the pan carefully to avoid breaking up the crab. Add the cream, Worcestershire sauce, and salt and pepper to taste.

Spoon the mixture into a buttered 3-cup ovenproof gratin dish or 6 individual ramekins. Sprinkle the top with cheese and bread crumbs and place under the broiler until golden brown, about 10 minutes. Decorate with parsley and a few small grilled shrimps, if desired.

Crab Mousse

4 portions

½ unwaxed cucumber
1½ envelopes (1½ tablespoons) unflavored gelatin
salt and freshly ground pepper
4 ounces cream cheese

8 ounces cooked crab meat, fresh, pasteurized or frozen
1 small green pepper
2 teaspoons lemon juice
½ cup light cream
paprika
few drops of Tabasco

Chill a 2-cup ring mold. Wash the cucumber, then grate it, including the skin, into a bowl. Soften ½ envelope of gelatin in 6 tablespoons cold water, or replace water with 2 tablespoons lemon juice or white-wine vinegar. When softened, set the pan over low heat and let the gelatin melt. Mix gelatin with cucumber and add salt and pepper to taste. Rinse the chilled mold with cold water and pour in the cucumber mixture, which will make a decorative pale-green layer when the mousse is unmolded.

Soften the whole envelope of gelatin in 6 tablespoons of water. Set the pan over low heat and let the gelatin melt. Soften the cream cheese in a bowl. Pick over the crab meat to remove any bits of shell or cartilage. Halve the green pepper, discard stem, seeds and ribs, and chop the pepper. Beat the crab meat, chopped pepper, lemon juice and cream into the cheese. Stir in the dissolved gelatin and add seasonings to taste, enough paprika to color the mixture, and the Tabasco. Make sure the mixture is well blended, then pour it onto the jelled cucumber layer and place in the refrigerator to set.

To turn out, dip the mold up to the rim into very hot water. Dry the mold, then invert on a serving dish and give the mold a sharp shake. It may be necessary to insert a thin knife blade at the edge to start the unmolding. Lift off the mold and wipe away any liquid that remains on the plate.

Fill the center of the ring with a fine-chopped mixture of lettuce and fresh herbs. If the mousse was molded in individual molds, turn them out on a bed of shredded lettuce. Serve triangles of brown bread and butter separately.

Lobster Bouchées

18 bouchées

18 baked Bouchée Cases, hot (see Volume 5 Index)
1 pound cooked lobster meat, fresh or frozen
8 ounces mushrooms
2 tablespoons butter
2 egg yolks
2 tablespoons heavy cream

1¼ cups Béchamel Sauce (see Volume 3 Index)
½ teaspoon salt
½ teaspoon black pepper
⅛ teaspoon cayenne pepper
½ cup medium-dry sherry
2 teaspoons lemon juice

Lift the centers from the bouchées and scoop out any soft pastry; keep the cases warm. Dice the lobster. Wipe mushrooms with a damp cloth and trim base of stems; slice caps and stems. Melt the butter in a frying pan over moderate heat. Add the mushrooms and sauté, stirring occasionally, for 5 to 6 minutes. Remove mushrooms with a slotted spoon and set them aside on a plate. Beat the egg yolks and cream together with a wire whisk.

Pour the béchamel sauce into a saucepan and set over moderate heat. Add the diced lobster, sautéed mushrooms, salt, pepper and cayenne. Cook the sauce, stirring carefully, for 2 to 3 minutes. Do not worry if the sauce is quite thick at this stage. Remove pan from heat and carefully stir in the egg-yolk and cream liaison. Return pan to low heat and cook the sauce gently, stirring constantly, for 2 minutes. Stir in the sherry and lemon juice and cook for 1 minute. Taste, and add more seasoning if necessary.

Spoon the filling into the hot bouchée cases and serve at once.

Mussels in Curried Mayonnaise

4 to 6 portions

40 mussels	⅔ cup mayonnaise
2 shallots	1 tablespoon minced fresh parsley
1 tablespoon olive oil	
1 tablespoon butter	4 to 6 cup-shaped lettuce leaves
1 teaspoon curry powder	
2 teaspoons lemon juice	

Scrub and debeard the mussels. Steam with liquid and flavoring vegetables (see Volume 7 Index) until the shells open. Remove mussels from their shells and discard shells, as well as any that have not opened. Filter the mussel liquid into a clean saucepan and simmer for 5 minutes to reduce it. Set aside.

Peel and mince the shallots. Heat oil and butter in a small saucepan and sauté shallots until translucent. Add curry powder and cook and stir until the curry darkens and begins to release its characteristic odor. Add the lemon juice and ¼ cup of the reduced mussel liquid. Simmer the mixture, stirring, until liquid is reduced to half. Cool it.

Spoon mayonnaise into a large bowl; add parsley and cooled curry mixture and stir with a wooden spoon until blended. If the sauce is too thick, add more mussel liquid, 1 teaspoon at a time. Turn the mussels into the mayonnaise and mix gently. Divide the mixture among the lettuce leaves on individual plates.

Variations: The mussels and mayonnaise are delicious served in avocado halves. The curry mayonnaise is equally good with shrimps or poached fish. Store any mussel liquid in the freezer for such uses.

Clams Casino

4 to 6 portions

24 cherrystone clams	1 tablespoon butter
rock salt	4 to 6 tablespoons fresh white bread crumbs
3 scallions	
8 parsley sprigs	4 slices of lean bacon
3 drops of Tabasco	4 to 6 lemon wedges

Shuck the clams, discard the top shells, and loosen the clams from the bottom shells, but leave them in place. Make a layer of rock salt in a large baking pan, or 2 pans if needed, and press the clams into the salt until steady and level. Preheat oven to 450°F.

Wash and trim scallions and cut into 1-inch lengths. Wash and dry parsley, including the stems, and cut into 1-inch lengths. Drop both into the bowl of a food processor fitted with the steel blade and process until reduced to small pieces; do not purée the vegetables, just mince them. At the

last second add the Tabasco. Melt the butter in a small saucepan and scrape the vegetables into it. Cook for 2 minutes. Remove from heat and mix in the bread crumbs. Cut each bacon strip into 6 squares.

Divide the crumb mixture among the clams, placing a scant teaspoon on each one. Place a bacon square on top. Slide the pan or pans into the oven and bake for about 12 minutes, until the bacon pieces are crisp. With tongs transfer clams to individual plates and serve at once, with lemon wedges.

Scallops Sautéed with Garlic and Basil

6 portions

1½ pounds sea scallops	3 garlic cloves
juice of ½ lemon	6 tablespoons vegetable oil
¼ teaspoon salt	¼ teaspoon dried basil
¼ teaspoon white pepper	2 tablespoons butter
½ cup flour	1 tablespoon chopped fresh parsley
3 shallots	

Rinse the scallops with room-temperature water, then dry on paper towels. Cut scallops into ½-inch pieces and place them on a sheet of wax paper. Sprinkle the lemon juice, salt and pepper over them. Put scallops in a strainer and sprinkle the flour over them. Shake the strainer over the sink, so the scallops are evenly covered with flour and excess flour goes through the strainer. Peel and mince the shallots; peel garlic cloves and put them through a press.

Heat 3 tablespoons of the oil in a large heavy frying pan over moderate heat. The oil should cover the pan with a thin film; if necessary add more. Add the scallops to the pan and toss them lightly with a wooden spoon. Cook for 5 minutes, until scallops are lightly browned. Add more oil during sautéing if pan seems at all dry. Add the shallots, garlic and basil to the pan and cook for another 2 minutes. Remove pan from heat, stir in the butter and parsley, and transfer scallops to 6 individual serving dishes that have been warmed. Serve immediately.

Sole-Stuffed Artichokes

4 portions

4 cooked large artichokes	1 cup dry white wine
4 sole or flounder fillets, 1 pound altogether	4 ounces mushrooms
½ teaspoon salt	2 tablespoons butter
½ teaspoon white pepper	1 cup Béchamel Sauce, hot (see Volume 3 Index)
½ teaspoon lemon juice	

Use tongs to lift artichokes from the cooking liquid and drain them upside down in a colander, then on paper towels. When cool enough to handle, remove most of the leaves, all the prickly center leaves and the hairy choke. You will have 4 saucer-shaped bottoms with a small rim of leaves. Place the artichokes in a pan of warm water to keep them hot until ready to use.

Place the fillets on a sheet of wax paper and sprinkle them with salt, white pepper and lemon juice. Roll up the fillets in jelly-roll fashion and fasten with white thread or small skewers. Place fillets in a small saucepan and pour in the white wine. Set pan over low heat and poach the rolled fillets for 5 to 8 minutes, basting occasionally if the rolls are not covered with the wine. Remove pan from heat and lift the sole from the liquid with a slotted spoon. Remove and discard the thread or skewers and keep the fillets warm until ready to use.

Wipe the mushrooms with a damp cloth, trim base of stems, and cut caps and stems into thin slices. Melt the butter in a small skillet over moderate heat. Add the mushrooms and cook, stirring occasionally, for 2 to 3 minutes. Remove pan from heat and set aside.

Drain artichoke bottoms and pat dry. Place them on a heated serving dish. Divide the mushrooms among the bottoms and spoon about ¼ cup of the béchamel sauce into each one. Place a roll of fish on top. Serve immediately.

Seviche of Scallops

Seviche is a famous South American dish in which raw fish are "cooked" by marination instead of heat. There are many versions. Scallop seviche is one of the most delicious.

6 portions

1 pound bay scallops
1 large mild-flavored onion
2 teaspoons crushed red
   pepper
4 black peppercorns
1 large bay leaf
½ cup fresh lime or lemon juice

1 small head of Boston lettuce
1 large red bell pepper
1 tablespoon chopped fresh parsley
2 tablespoons olive oil
   salt and pepper
   additional lime juice or
      white-wine vinegar

Rinse scallops, roll in paper towels to dry, and place them in a glass container, making an even layer. Peel and slice the onion and separate the slices into rings. Arrange onion rings on the scallops and sprinkle with the crushed red pepper. Crack peppercorns in a mortar and break the bay leaf into small pieces; sprinkle these over the scallops. Pour in the lime or lemon juice; if it does not cover the scallops, turn them over so all sides are moistened. Cover the container with plastic wrap and refrigerate for at least 8 hours. Turn the scallops over at least twice during the marinating.

Wash and dry lettuce and shred or tear into rough pieces. Divide among 6 salad plates. Wash and halve the bell pepper, discard stem, seeds and ribs, and chop the pepper. When the scallops have been "cooked" by the acid of the fruit juice, lift them out to a bowl. Add the chopped bell pepper, parsley and olive oil and sprinkle with a little salt and pepper. Mix gently. Taste; add more seasoning if needed; if the flavor is not piquant enough, add a little fresh lime juice or white-wine vinegar. Divide the scallop mixture among the lettuce-lined plates. Serve cold or at room temperature.

Variations: The same procedure can be used for weakfish, flounder, mackerel, or a combination of all three. Cut the raw fish into 1-inch strips before marinating.

Seafood Timbales

(Savory Seafood Custards)

6 portions

3   tablespoons unsalted butter
1½ pounds cooked white fish
       and shellfish (flounder,
       cod, crab, shrimp, lobster)
2   scallions
1   teaspoon curry powder
1   tablespoon flour

2 large eggs
½ cup milk
3 tablespoons chopped canned
      pimiento
1 tablespoon lemon juice
   salt and pepper

Use 1 tablespoon of the butter to coat 6 timbale molds or ½-cup custard cups or ramekins. Preheat oven to 325°F. Pick over fish and shellfish to remove any bones, bits of shell or cartilage. Chop all the various kinds into small pieces. Wash and trim the scallions and chop both green and white parts. Heat remaining butter in a small pan and cook scallions until tender. Stir in curry powder and flour and cook, stirring, until the mixture begins to change color. Beat eggs and milk together in a bowl. Off the heat, pour the egg mixture into the curry mixture, stirring all the time, until blended. Simmer over low heat for 2 minutes. Remove from heat and stir in the chopped shellfish, pimiento and lemon juice; mix well. Taste, and add seasoning if needed.

Spoon the mixture into the buttered molds. Set them in a large pan of hot water. Bake in the center of the oven for 25 to 30 minutes. Insert a skewer or a small thin knife halfway between the center and the edge of the mold; if it comes out clean, carefully remove the timbales from the oven. Let them sit for a few minutes, then serve in the molds, or turn out on individual plates.

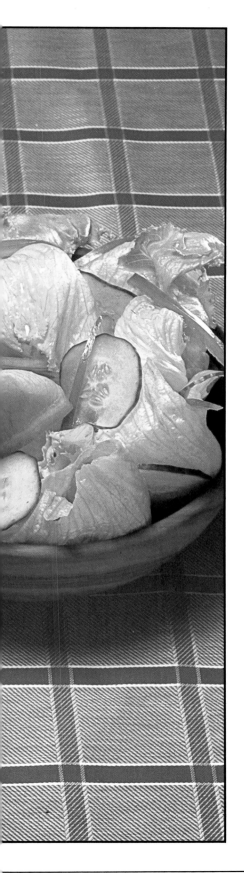

Part Two
GROUND MEAT

"They [the Chinese] cut the meat into very small particles, and then put it into a pickle of salt, with the addition of several of their spices. It is thus prepared for persons of the higher class, but the poorer sort only steep it, after mincing, in a sauce of garlic, and then eat it as if it were dressed."

—*The Travels of Marco Polo*

During the thirteenth century, Kublai Khan ruled over a vast domain that stretched from China westward into Europe and from the Arctic south into India, Burma and Siam. Fierce Tartar warriors galloped across the oceanic sweep of Asian steppes on mighty steeds—horses, some claimed, that were descendants of Alexander the Great's beloved Bucephalus. Their custom was to carry a slab of freshly butchered meat, tucked safely in between horse and saddle and thus constantly pounded, in the course of a hard day's ride. At mealtime the meat thus tenderized was scraped and shredded until it was finely minced; then it was seasoned with onion, garlic and a little salt.

Some 600 years later Brillat-Savarin, the famous gastronome, tells about a Croat officer who said to him, "When we are in the field and are hungry we kill the first beast we come upon; we cut ourselves a good meaty slice of it, sprinkle it with some salt . . . put it between our saddle and the back of the horse, and give it a good gallop. Then . . . we feast as well as any prince." (*The Physiology of Taste.*)

Although steak tartare, as it has come to be called, is not to everyone's taste, there are many people who dote on this chopped beef dish, and they are as fussy about the way it is prepared as they are convinced that raw meat is a palliative for hangovers, a healthful stimulant, an aphrodisiac, a general restorative for tired bodies, minds and spirits. Scraping and shredding the beef is still the preferred method of obtaining a fine mince, and the seasonings of finely chopped onions, salt and pepper remain classically true to the original Tartare dish. Only the addition of a little finely chopped fresh parsley, a dollop of mustard, a perfect egg yolk and a dash of Cognac is permitted by the connoisseur, although bell peppers, anchovies, and capers are equally delicious additions.

The German city of Hamburg on the river Elbe was once a bustling center of trade and commerce. Its merchants traveled to the Baltic and beyond and it is thought that it was by this route that steak tartare was introduced to Europe. The Europeans, not accustomed to eating their meat raw, cooked the minced meat patties and so the hamburg steak was born. Like so many other dishes of foreign birth, the hamburg steak was brought to America by German immigrants in the nineteenth century. The first hamburger as we know it, the broiled meat patty in a bun, was served at the St. Louis World's Fair in 1903, and thus was introduced one of the most ubiquitous items in the history of American cuisine.

In a television report about America's eating habits, Charles Kuralt stated that in 1969 Americans had eaten forty billion hamburgers, "give or take a few hundred million," and he described his travels in the following terms:

"You can find your way across this country using burger joints the way a navigator uses stars. . . . We have munched bridge burgers in the shadow of Brooklyn Bridge and Cable burgers hard by the Golden Gate, Dixie burgers in the sunny South and Yankee Doodle burgers in the North. . . . We had a Capitol burger—guess where. And so help us, in the inner courtyard of the Pentagon, a Penta burger. . . . We've had grabba burgers, kinga burgers, lotta burgers, castle burgers, country burgers, bronco burgers, Broadway burgers, broiled burgers, beefnut burgers, prime burgers, flame burgers . . . dude burgers, char burgers, tall boy burgers, golden burgers, 747 jet burgers, whiz burgers, nifty burgers, and thing burgers. . . ." (Quoted in *American Food,* by Evan Jones.)

If by virtue of its popularity and great variety the hamburger lays claim to being called the all-American food, then meatballs, though they appear around the world, belong most properly to the cooking of the Middle East. "Behind the seemingly inexhaustible range of subtly varying and intriguing ground meatballs," writes Claudia Roden, "one can discern the creative spirit responsible for the luscious designs which decorate Arab pottery, carpets, and minarets. It inspired in cookery a rhythmic and prolific repetition as it did the floral and geometric patterns, endless variations on a theme. Each district and each town has striven to offer its own particular specialty for a meatball." (*A Book of Middle Eastern Food.*)

Ground meats in general, of course, are the foundation of some of the most popular dishes in every country in the world. They are the mainstay of bourgeois cuisine—wonderful food prepared at home to feed the family and friends. Ground beef, veal, lamb, pork and even chicken or turkey—in splendid combinations or simply on their own—make up a repertory of cosy, comforting, delicious dishes that never cease to please, satisfy and then surprise us with their infinite variety. It would be difficult indeed to find a national cuisine that does not have a treasure trove of ground meat specialties—its *fricadelles;* its shepherd's pie and *moussaka; chili con carne, chicken pojarski; kofta, keftedes, albondigas, königsberger klops; picadillo* and tamale pie; meat loaves and sloppy joes, meatballs and Salisbury steak. The list is various and endless and reflects the fact that clever and resourceful cooks around the world all know a good thing when they see it.

The cheaper, tougher cuts of meat tend to be more flavorful as well, so they are the very cuts that can be ground or minced or finely chopped—whether by grinder, food processor or even with a knife—to best advantage. The meat is tender, delicious, economical and versatile indeed. For a novice cook as well as for the seasoned chef, the world of ground meat cookery provides a multitude of satisfactions.

GROUND MEATS

Ground meat, either raw or cooked, is the key to making interesting low-cost meals. Although good-quality meat can be used, one advantage of ground meat is that the grinding process is a means of tenderizing tough cuts. The connective tissue is broken up, making the meat more tender and palatable. It is also faster to cook, which is a convenience.

Meat can be ground coarse or fine; a finer grind is recommended for tough cuts of meat. Coarse-ground meat retains more of its natural flavor and produces dishes with a fairly rough texture. Fine-ground meat, although smoother and more tender, loses more flavor during the grinding process. It binds and holds together more easily than coarse-ground meat, but needs more spices and piquant sauces to compensate for the loss of flavor. Cooking methods for ground meat can be either fast or slow—quick grilling or broiling of a hamburger or slow cooking of a thick sauce.

Buying Ground Meat

Ground meat is extremely perishable and preferably should be used on the day it is bought. It can be stored in the refrigerator for a day or two, but no longer. If frozen, it should not be kept for longer than 2 or 3 weeks. It is much better and safer to freeze meat in cubes or chunks rather than in its ground form. There is a great potential for bacterial infection from ground meat, because of the many surfaces that result from grinding, which is the reason for the strict recommendations on its storage. Also, the meat can lose juices and flavor if kept longer than a day or two.

If you are buying ground meat from the butcher, it is best to select the cut of meat you want and ask the butcher to grind it for you. However, this is not always possible. In the case of pork, for example, there are regulations that prohibit pork being ground in the same machine used for other meats unless the machine is taken apart and cleaned thoroughly before any other meat is ground in it. This is done as a precaution to prevent the occurrence of trichinosis, a very real and constant danger when dealing with raw pork. Butchers who grind pork normally keep a separate grinder for it.

Color is a good indicator of the freshness of ground meat. Ground beef should have a healthy red color, and veal and lamb should be pinkish. Beware of any ground meat that looks grayish or brownish.

The fineness of the grind is easily discernible. As for fat content, fat shows up in little white pieces; the meatier-looking the ground meat appears, the leaner it will be.

Ground beef, the meat used for hamburgers, is seldom sold today under the name "hamburger." The label on ground beef should list the wholesale cut from which the meat was cut (chuck, sirloin, round, etc.) and the percentage of fat in the meat. According to federal regulations in the United States, ground beef may not contain more than 30 percent fat; the beef is ground twice (ideally hamburger meat should be ground only once); and it may contain portions from different parts of the animal, to make it more flavorful. Leaner ground beef will list the percentage of fat, in addition to being labeled as lean.

Grinding Your Own

The best way to insure the freshness and control the leanness of the meat is to grind your own, with either a meat grinder or a food processor. This way the meat can be ground at the last minute and its freshness will be assured.

Choose the cut according to the cooking method you plan to use. For broiling or barbecuing, buy a mixture of chuck and sirloin. For panfrying buy

Decorative Potato Toppings

1 For a fancy topping for a savory pie, pipe a line around the outside of the pie using a size 12 fluted tube.

2 Continue piping lines in decreasing circles until all of the pie is covered.

sirloin, not round, as round lacks fat and the patties made from this cut would be dry. Ground chuck alone is flavorful and has a good balance of fat and lean.

Veal, pork and lamb, which are less often sold already ground, are slaughtered when so young that all the cuts are tender, especially after grinding. Lamb shoulder is the best cut for lamb patties; other portions are too lean. Pork shoulder is also a good choice for grinding for meat loaf mixtures or for meatballs. Veal should be ground from shin, neck and shoulder to have adequate moisture and flavor. Do not plan to broil or barbecue veal alone as the meat is too lean and dry; however, it adds good flavor and gelatin to a mixture with other meats.

Preparation

Before grinding raw meat, remove skin, gristle and excess fat. Wipe the meat with a damp towel and cut it into cubes for grinding.

For very fine meat, put it through the grinder twice, or process longer in the food processor.

Remove all bones from cooked meat and cut into cubes for grinding.

Additions to Ground Meat

The addition of other ingredients, which makes a little meat go a long way, also increases the protein and nutritional value. These include bread, pasta, and cooked dried beans. Bread can be fresh, toasted or crumbed. Stale bread can be soaked in milk or stock to soften it. Bread crumbs can be mixed with the meat, used in layers, used as a coating for fried meat patties, or used as a topping, sometimes combined with cheese.

Potatoes are often used with ground meat, usually in mashed form, but sometimes diced, as in hash. In mashed form they are combined with meat to form a cake, used as a topping, or piped around the meat as a decorative border. Sliced, parboiled potatoes are often layered into the meat.

Grated or minced vegetables extend the meat and add flavor and vitamins. Grated carrots are popular because they add moisture and do not have an overpowering flavor. A more flavorsome mixture is the classic one of gently sautéing minced onion, carrot and celery together before adding the meat.

Pasta and rice are traditional extenders in Italian cooking.

When using already cooked meat, there are a few points to remember. First, the meat will have lost much of its natural juices and may be a bit dry. Therefore moisture has to be added to the dish in the form of a sauce, gravy or moist vegetables. The meat will also have lost some of its flavor; this can be compensated for by the use of herbs, spices, wine and piquant sauces. Raw ingredients, such as onion or garlic, can be ground along with the meat. Cooked vegetables can be added during the cooking.

Binding Ground Meat

The method of binding varies according to the texture required, the degree of fineness of the ground meat.

When a loose texture is required, as for hamburgers—one of the advan-

OR Cover the pie with rosettes using a size 6 star tube. Squeeze, lift and repeat. Try to make all the rosettes the same size and shape.

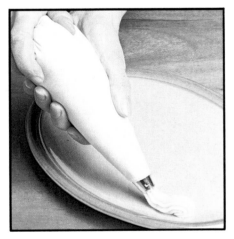

1 For a fancy border use a size 8 star tube. Hold the bag away from you and squeeze out 1 inch of purée.

2 Keeping the tube close to the dish, squeeze again, then lift so that a scallop shape is formed by the purée.

Making Hamburgers

1 Trim any skin or gristle from the meat. Cut meat into cubes and chop or grind it once or twice.

2 Season meat with salt and pepper. Turn it out on a flat surface; divide into 4-ounce portions.

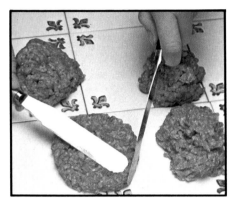

3 Using a spatula, flatten each portion lightly and shape it into a round ¾ inch thick.

4 Heat 1 tablespoon oil in a heavy skillet. When hot, add hamburgers in a single layer.

5 Panfry for 3 to 4 minutes per side for a medium-rare hamburger. Turn only once. Be careful not to break up the patty.

6 Lift from pan, add desired topping, and serve in a warm or toasted bun.

Shaping Meatballs

1 The meat must be ground very fine. Trim and cube it and grind 2 or 3 times.

2 Combine meat with flavorings and extending ingredients and add a beaten egg.

3 Beat firmly with a wooden spoon to bind the ingredients thoroughly. Turn out on a lightly floured surface.

tages of custom-grinding your own meat, or having the butcher do it, is being able to select the best grind for a recipe—the meat is ground coarse and the only binding agent is the meat juices. The juices coagulate in the cooking and hold the particles together. This bind, however, would not be sufficient to hold during a long period of cooking.

When a smooth texture is required, as for meatballs, the meat is ground fine, sometimes as many as 3 times. The smaller particles of meat hold together more readily than the coarse-ground meats, and will stay intact during cooking without an added binding agent.

The most common method of binding ground meats is to use beaten egg. The egg proteins coagulate on contact with heat and hold the ingredients together. Egg is needed when other ingredients, such as bread crumbs or rice, have been mixed with the meat before shaping. Another sure way of binding ground meat is with a very thick sauce, either a béchamel (made with milk) or a velouté (made with stock) (see Volume 3 Index). The proportions should be 1 cup sauce for 2 cups ground meat. The sauce should

be made of 3 tablespoons butter or margarine, 3 tablespoons flour and 1 cup liquid. This is the sauce to use to bind cooked meat for forming into croquettes.

Shaping Ground Meat

The usual and best method of shaping is with the hands, dampened by dipping into cold water. Cold water helps prevent the mixture sticking to the hands.

Ground meat is formed into varied shapes—balls, round flat patties, pyramid-shaped croquettes, sausage-shaped rolls, loaves, etc.

Cooking Ground Meat

Fresh ground meat always includes a certain proportion of fat. This is unavoidable, but it has the bonus of keeping the meat tender and juicy. It also means that very little extra fat is needed in the cooking process. The pan is merely greased with enough fat to prevent sticking; the frying is brief and done over high heat. The fat can be butter, oil, margarine, or meat or bacon

drippings. Onion, garlic and herbs are often cooked first to add flavor.

Cooked ground meat does not need to be browned but it does need to be thoroughly heated. Raw vegetables, such as onion or pepper, are cooked first until soft. A small amount of liquid (or a liquid vegetable such as tomato) is simmered with the vegetables for a moment before the cooked meat is added.

Cooked meat is particularly useful for stuffing vegetables, such as zucchini, eggplant, and peppers.

Hamburgers

A true hamburger is made from good-quality lean beef, ground once or twice and not ground too fine. When cooked, a hamburger should be thick and juicy. The average size is 4 ounces. When served in a warm or toasted bun, this is sufficient for most appetites. There is no ham or pork of any kind in a hamburger; the name comes from the city of Hamburg in northern Germany.

The surest way to get the right meat is to buy boneless beef of the cut of your choice and grind it at home. Hamburger meat should hold together when shaped. However, when mixing and shaping it, handle the meat as little as possible to avoid compacting it. The juices that coagulate during cooking will hold the burger in shape.

All hamburgers can be broiled or panfried rare, medium or well done. The meat can be seasoned with pepper before it is shaped. Salt is also added, as it encourages the juices to run. This is contrary to the usual process of frying, in which salt is not recommended until after the surface is browned. Barbecued hamburgers need a little more fat; when the meat is just right, they can be barbecued to any degree of doneness.

Meatballs

While hamburgers are considered an American dish in spite of their true origin, meatballs hail from the Middle East. Meatballs can be made from beef or lamb or from a combination of beef,

 4 Roll a spoonful of the mixture firmly between lightly floured hands to form a ball.

OR Roll each portion with one hand against a floured surface, forming a ball.

Steak Tartare

4 portions

1 medium-size onion
½ small green pepper
½ small red pepper
1 pound raw beef fillet, sirloin or round steak
  salt and freshly ground black pepper
4 large egg yolks
8 anchovy fillets
4 tablespoons capers
  chopped parsley

1 Assemble a meat grinder, using the fine grind blade. Or fit a food processor with the steel blade.

2 Peel and mince the onion. Wash peppers, discard stems, seeds and ribs, and chop.

3 Trim any fat from the meat. Wipe with a damp paper towel and cut into cubes.

4 Grind meat, a few cubes at a time, pushing them through with a wooden spoon. Grind twice.

OR Grinding 1 cup of firmly packed cubes at a time, put meat in processor bowl and pulse until desired texture has been reached.

5 Season meat generously with salt and pepper. Divide into 4 portions and place them on chilled plates.

6 Shape the meat into a round and make an indentation in the center of each.

7 Garnish with an egg yolk, anchovies, capers, parsley, and chopped peppers.

lamb, pork and veal. The important thing to remember is that whatever meat is used, it needs to be fairly lean and it must be ground very fine so the ground meat clings together and holds its shape.

Meatballs are made smaller than hamburgers and are rolled more firmly. The meat is ground 2 or 3 times through the fine blades of the grinder and is then divided into portions with a spoon. Meatballs can be as small as a marble. The portions are then shaped into balls with the hands or by rolling under the palm of the hand against a flat surface. The surface should be dampened or floured to prevent sticking.

Meatballs will hold their shape without a binding agent, but, when extending ingredients such as rice, bread, cracked wheat or potatoes are added to the meat, an egg can be used to hold the mixture together.

Flavoring meatballs. Meatballs are often served highly spiced, due to their Middle Eastern heritage, in which spices are used abundantly. Allspice, cinnamon, cuminseed, ginger, coriander and nutmeg are among the spices used. Grated onion, garlic, herbs, pine nuts, seedless raisins and tomato purée are other favorite additions.

Cooking meatballs. One reason for their popularity must be their versatility. Meatballs can be fried, broiled, baked, simmered in a sauce or poached in water and then finished in a sauce or fried or broiled.

Meatballs are fried or broiled in the same way as hamburgers and other minced meat shapes. The heat should be high and a minimum of cooking fat is used. The balls should be turned frequently to insure even browning. Cooking time is brief as the shapes are small, but they should be cooked through. Ten minutes is the average time needed, but increase or decrease according to size.

When the meatballs are simmered or poached, they are added to hot sauce or water. The heat is reduced to simmering point or just below and the meatballs are cooked for 10 to 20 minutes, according to their size.

Curried Beef and Mushrooms

4 portions

1 medium-size onion
1 or 2 garlic cloves
1 celery rib
2 tablespoons oil or beef
  drippings

12 ounces ground beef
5 tablespoons flour
½ cup beef broth
2 tablespoons tomato paste
2 teaspoons curry powder
4 ounces mushrooms

1 cup plain yogurt
2 large eggs
  salt and black pepper
2 ounces Cheddar cheese
  (¼ cup grated)

1 Peel and mince the onion and garlic. Wash and mince the celery.

2 Melt oil or drippings in a heavy pan and brown the meat over low heat.

3 Add the vegetables and cook, stirring, until they are soft but not browned.

4 Stir in 1 tablespoon flour. Cook for 2 minutes, blending well, and then add the broth, tomato paste and curry powder.

5 Simmer gently for 5 minutes. Wipe mushrooms with a damp cloth, slice, and add them to the pan.

6 Transfer to a flat baking dish. Preheat oven to 375°F.

7 Place yogurt in a bowl. Beat eggs and stir into yogurt. Beat in remaining 4 tablespoons flour.

8 Sprinkle meat mixture with salt and pepper. Add cheese to the yogurt mixture. Pour on top of meat to cover.

9 Bake for 30 minutes, until topping has set and is golden brown.

Moussaka

8 to 10 portions

3 eggplants, 1 pound each	¼ teaspoon grated nutmeg
salt	¼ teaspoon ground cinnamon
1 cup minced onion	black pepper
¾ cup olive or cooking oil	½ cup bread crumbs
2 pounds lean lamb, ground	2 cups Béchamel Sauce (see
1 cup chopped peeled	Volume 3 Index)
tomatoes, fresh or canned	2 ounces Parmesan cheese,
4 tablespoons minced parsley	grated (½ cup)
1 cup dry red or white wine, or	
beef stock (see Volume 1	
Index)	

Peel the eggplants and cut them lengthwise into slices about ½ inch thick. Sprinkle slices with salt and let them drain in a colander for at least 30 minutes. Meanwhile sauté the onion in ¼ cup of the oil for a few minutes, until limp. Add the lamb and brown it over low heat. Add the tomatoes, parsley, wine or stock, the spices, and pepper to taste. Mix well and simmer for about 45 minutes.

Drain the eggplant slices and pat dry. Sauté the slices quickly on both sides in a little oil. Remove from pan and drain on paper towels. Continue until all the slices are sautéed, adding oil as necessary. Add the bread crumbs to the meat sauce and let sauce cool slightly. Preheat oven to 375°F.

Oil a baking dish, about 9 × 12 × 2 inches, and place a layer of eggplant slices in the dish. Spread with half of the meat sauce. Add another layer of eggplant slices, and top with remaining meat sauce. Cover with the béchamel sauce and top with the grated cheese. Bake in the oven for 45 to 50 minutes.

Let the moussaka cool for about 20 minutes before cutting into squares. Serve it warm rather than hot.

Hungarian Meatball Goulash

6 to 8 portions

3 garlic cloves
4 slices of rye bread
3 tablespoons milk
1 egg
1 pound lean beef, ground
1 pound lean pork, ground
1½ teaspoons salt
1 teaspoon black pepper
1½ teaspoons dried dill
½ teaspoon cayenne pepper
1 teaspoon grated orange rind

2 medium-size onions
2 carrots
4 ounces mushrooms
¼ cup vegetable oil
1½ tablespoons paprika
1½ cups beef stock
½ cup red wine
1 teaspoon caraway seeds
4 large potatoes
2 teaspoons cornstarch
1¼ cups sour cream

Peel the garlic cloves; put 2 cloves through a press into a large bowl; crush the third and set aside. Remove crusts from rye bread and soak the slices in the milk for 5 minutes. Beat the egg. Add soaked bread, the egg, beef, pork, 1 teaspoon salt, ½ teaspoon pepper, 1 teaspoon dill, the cayenne and orange rind to the bowl. Mix until thoroughly blended. Form into small balls. Refrigerate, covered, for about 30 minutes.

Peel and chop onions. Scrape carrots and slice into rounds. Wipe mushrooms with a damp cloth and trim base of stems; slice caps and stems. In a large pan, heat the oil; when hot, add the onions, crushed garlic and carrots, and cook, stirring, for 5 to 7 minutes, until onions are soft but not browned. Add the mushrooms and paprika and cook for about 3 minutes. Pour in the stock and wine and add remaining salt, pepper and dill, and the caraway seeds. Bring to a boil.

Remove meatballs from refrigerator and add to the pan. Let the liquids come to a boil, lower the heat and simmer, covered, for 1 hour.

Peel and quarter the potatoes. Uncover the pan and add the potatoes. Cover the pan again and simmer for 20 minutes, until the potatoes are cooked through. Mix cornstarch with 1 tablespoon water. Uncover the pan and stir in the cornstarch mixture and the sour cream. Cook, stirring constantly, for 2 or 3 minutes, until sauce has thickened and is hot. Do not let it boil. Serve at once.

Egg Noodles with Pork Sauce

4 portions

1 large cucumber	2 tablespoons Worcestershire sauce
3 scallions	1 tablespoon soy sauce
1 or 2 garlic cloves	2 teaspoons brown sugar
1 large onion	6 tablespoons chicken stock
4 tablespoons vegetable oil	12 ounces egg noodles
1 pound lean pork, ground	2 teaspoons salt
2 tablespoons dry sherry	

Peel the cucumber and cut lengthwise into halves. Scoop out the seeds with the tip of a spoon. Cut cucumbers lengthwise into ¼-inch slices and cut these into 2-inch strips. Wash, trim, and mince the scallions. Peel and mince the garlic. Peel and mince the onion. Place cucumbers and scallions on a serving plate and set them aside for use as a garnish.

In a large frying pan over high heat, heat 3 tablespoons of the oil for about 1 minute, until very hot. Lower the heat to moderate and add the garlic; let the garlic cook for about 1 minute. Add the pork; cook, stirring constantly, for about 5 minutes, until the meat begins to brown. Stir in the sherry,

Worcestershire, soy sauce, minced onion, brown sugar and chicken stock. Bring to a boil and cook over moderate heat for 10 to 15 minutes, until all the liquid has evaporated.

Meanwhile, bring a large pot of water to a boil. When the liquid has evaporated from the pork sauce, cover the pan and remove it from heat; keep warm while the noodles cook. Place the noodles in the boiling water with the salt. Cook just until tender, 6 to 8 minutes. Drain and toss with remaining oil. Place noodles on a heated serving dish and cover with the pork sauce. Serve with a side dish of the cucumbers and scallions.

Curried Lamb Burgers

4 to 6 portions

1½ pounds lean lamb, ground	½ cup fine bread crumbs
1 egg	2 tablespoons chopped parsley
½ cup minced onion	salt and pepper
1 tablespoon vegetable oil	2 tablespoons butter
1 to 2 teaspoons curry powder	mango chutney

Place the lamb in a mixing bowl. Beat the egg to blend lightly. In a small pan, sauté the onion in the oil until wilted. Add the curry powder and cook for a minute or two. Remove from heat and stir in the bread crumbs. Combine this mixture with the ground lamb and stir in the beaten egg and chopped parsley. Season with salt and pepper to taste. Divide the mixture into 12 portions. Form the portions into balls and flatten them to make patties.

Melt the butter in a large heavy skillet and sauté the burgers for 3 to 4 minutes on each side. As they are sautéed, remove them to a heated platter while continuing to sauté the rest. Serve with chutney on the side.

Classic Meat Loaf

6 portions

1 pound ground beef
8 ounces veal, ground
8 ounces lean pork, ground
2 eggs
½ cup fine bread crumbs
½ cup chopped parsley
¼ cup minced onion
¼ cup chopped green pepper (optional)
1½ teaspoons salt
½ teaspoon freshly ground pepper
¼ teaspoon dried orégano or marjoram
bacon slices for top
2 medium-size tomatoes for garnish
8 pimiento-stuffed green olives for garnish

Preheat oven to 350°F. Lightly beat eggs. In a mixing bowl combine all the ingredients except the bacon. Blend well (your hands are best for this), but do not overwork the mixture. Line a loaf pan with aluminum foil, pack the meat into it, and cover the top with bacon. Bake for 1½ hours. Let cool for at least 15 minutes before serving. Discard the bacon. Cut tomatoes and olives crosswise into ¼-inch slices and garnish the meat loaf. Or serve loaf with tomato sauce.

Chickenburgers

6 portions

2 pounds boneless raw chicken, ground (preferably breast meat)
½ teaspoon salt
¼ teaspoon freshly ground pepper
¼ cup minced parsley

1 cup fresh bread crumbs
1 teaspoon dried tarragon
¼ cup cream or chicken stock
4 tablespoons butter, or 2 tablespoons butter and 2 tablespoons oil

Combine all the ingredients except butter in a mixing bowl, and blend well with your hands. Divide the mixture into 12 portions. Dampen your hands and form 12 flat patties. Refrigerate for at least 1 hour.

Heat the butter in a heavy skillet just until it starts to bubble. Cook the chicken patties for about 4 minutes on each side. Transfer to a heated serving platter.
Turkey may be substituted for the chicken.

Variations: In another pan, sauté sliced mushrooms. When the chicken patties are cooked, deglaze the pan with ½ cup dry white wine and quickly boil it until reduced by half. Pour this over the mushrooms and swirl in a few small pieces of butter or a little heavy cream. Heat through and pour over patties.

Chili Con Carne

4 to 5 portions

1 cup red kidney beans or two 16-ounce cans
salt
1 pound onions (about 2 medium)
5 cloves
5 garlic cloves
1 bay leaf
1 teaspoon dried orégano

6 large dried chilies, preferably 3 ancho and 3 pasíl, or 2 to 3 tablespoons chili powder
1 medium-size red pepper
4 teaspoons oil
1½ pounds ground chuck
1 teaspoon cumin (if using dried chilies)

If using dried beans, pick over them and rinse briefly. Bring 6 cups of water and 1½ teaspoons salt to a boil. Add beans, stir, and quickly return water to the boil. Boil beans for 2 minutes. Cover pan, remove from heat, and leave for 1 hour.

Peel 1 onion and stud with cloves. Peel 3 garlic cloves and add them to the beans along with the onion, bay leaf, and orégano. If necessary, add water to bring level of liquid to ½ inch above beans. Bring to a simmer, reduce heat to very low, and cook approximately 1½ hours or until tender, adding water from time to time if needed. Be careful not to overcook.

If using dried chilies, about ½ hour before the beans are ready, place the chilies in a heavy, dry skillet and toast them over medium heat 1 to 2 minutes or until fragrant. Watch carefully to prevent them from burning.

Wearing rubber gloves, clean chilies, removing stem, seeds, and veins. Rinse chilies and place in hot water to cover

for about 20 minutes or until soft. (If chilies are very brittle, soak before cleaning.)

While the chilies are soaking, peel the remaining onions and garlic cloves and chop fine. Wash the red pepper, seed, devein, and dice.

Drain chilies, reserving soaking water, and purée in a blender, adding a little of the soaking water if necessary.

Heat the oil in a large heavy skillet set over medium heat. Sauté the onion and garlic for about 5 minutes or until translucent and beginning to soften.

Add the meat and stir to break up. When the meat has begun to brown, add puréed chilies and cumin, or chili powder, if using. (Add chili powder in small amounts, tasting after each addition until desired flavor is reached.) Add diced red pepper. Reduce heat to low and, stirring occasionally, cook over medium heat for about 10 minutes.

Drain the kidney beans (cooked or canned) and reserve

the liquid. Add beans to chili. Dissolve the tomato paste in 2 tablespoons of the reserved bean liquid and stir into the chili along with 1½ teaspoons salt. Cook at a gentle simmer for about 15 minutes, adding more of the reserved liquid if necessary. Taste for seasoning.

Turn chili into a deep serving dish and serve with boiled rice and a green salad.

Veal Patties with Cream and Cognac

4 to 6 portions

1½	pounds lean veal, ground	3	tablespoons soft butter
1	medium-size onion	1	egg
1	teaspoon salt		flour
	freshly ground pepper	2	tablespoons butter or oil
½	teaspoon dried tarragon	¾	cup heavy cream
⅔	cup fresh bread crumbs		juice of ½ lemon
¼	cup milk	1	tablespoon Cognac

Place the ground veal in a bowl. Peel and grate the onion and add to veal with salt, pepper to taste, and the tarragon. Soak the bread crumbs in the milk. Beat egg. Mash crumbs thoroughly with the soft butter and the egg. This can be done in a blender. Combine the bread-crumb mixture with the meat and beat vigorously until the mixture is smooth and light. With dampened hands, divide the mixture into 6 portions. Roll each portion into a ball and flatten to form patties about ½ inch thick. Refrigerate for 1 hour or longer.

Just before sautéing, sprinkle the patties lightly with flour and brush off excess. Heat the butter or oil until very hot and sauté the patties for 3 to 4 minutes on each side, until golden brown. Remove to a heated serving plate and keep warm while making the sauce.

Pour off the fat from the skillet and add the cream. Over high heat boil the cream until reduced by half. Add the lemon juice, salt and pepper to taste, and the Cognac. Heat briefly, then spoon sauce over the patties.

Sweet-and-Sour Meatballs

4 portions

1 egg
1 pound lean beef, ground fine
⅓ cup fresh bread crumbs
salt and pepper
3 tablespoons flour
1 small onion
1 large carrot
1 leek

2 celery ribs
3 large or 6 small mushrooms
3 tablespoons oil
2 teaspoons cornstarch
2 teaspoons sugar
1 tablespoon ketchup
1 tablespoon wine vinegar
2 teaspoons soy sauce

Beat egg. Combine ground beef, bread crumbs, egg, and salt and pepper to taste in a bowl. Add 1 tablespoon water and beat with a wooden spoon until thoroughly mixed. Turn the mixture onto a lightly floured surface and divide into 16 portions. Flour your hands and roll each portion between the palms to form a ball. Cover meatballs with wax paper and refrigerate while preparing the vegetables.

Peel and chop the onion. Scrape the carrot; slice lengthwise and then across into strips. Trim and wash the leek and slice crosswise into rounds. Wash and slice the celery. Wipe the mushrooms and halve or quarter them, according to size. Heat the oil in a large sauté pan with a

cover. When very hot, sauté the meatballs, in 2 batches if necessary, until browned all over. Remove with a slotted spoon and drain on paper towels. Place all the vegetables in the sauté pan, uncovered, and cook gently, stirring occasionally, for about 10 minutes.

Place cornstarch and sugar in a bowl and gradually stir in 1 cup water. Beat in the ketchup, vinegar and soy sauce. Pour this mixture over the vegetables in the pan and cook, stirring, until it comes to a boil. Return the meatballs to the pan, season to taste with salt and pepper, cover, and simmer over low heat for 30 minutes. Serve with noodles.

North African Meatballs

4 portions

¼ teaspoon thread saffron
2 tablespoons hot water
2 medium-size onions
2 pounds ground lamb shoulder
1 tablespoon chopped fresh parsley
1 teaspoon chopped fresh thyme
1 teaspoon salt
2 to 3 tablespoons butter
2 to 3 tablespoons oil

1 small potato
1 1-inch piece fresh gingerroot
1 teaspoon ground cumin
1 teaspoon ground coriander
½ teaspoon black pepper
½ teaspoon sugar
½ teaspoon chili powder
1 tablespoon white wine vinegar
1 tablespoon chopped fresh coriander leaves (optional)

Using a mortar and pestle, grind the thread saffron to a powder. Soak saffron in 2 tablespoons hot water for 30 minutes.

Peel and mince onion. Set half aside and combine remaining half with lamb, parsley, thyme, and ½ teaspoon salt. Knead just until well mixed. Shape meat into 36 balls about 1 inch in diameter.

In a large heavy skillet, melt 2 tablespoons butter with 2 tablespoons oil over medium heat. When the foam subsides add about one quarter of the meatballs and sauté, turning frequently, for 6 to 8 minutes, or until well browned. Using a slotted spoon, transfer meatballs to a paper-towel-lined plat-

ter and cover loosely with aluminum foil. Repeat the procedure with remaining meatballs until all have been browned.

Peel the potato and chop fine. If necessary, add more butter and oil to skillet in which meatballs were browned. Add potatoes and reserved onions, and cook, stirring occasionally, for 5 to 7 minutes or until onion is soft but not browned and the potato is almost tender. While potato is cooking, peel ginger and chop fine.

Add the ginger and cook, stirring occasionally, for 3 minutes. Add the cumin, coriander, pepper, sugar, chili powder, and the remaining salt and cook for 5 minutes, stirring frequently to prevent the spices from sticking to the bottom of the pan. Stir in the vinegar, the saffron water, and ¾ cup water. Let simmer for 2 minutes.

Return the meatballs to the pan and stir carefully to coat them with the spices. Adjust heat so liquid simmers gently,

cover pan, and cook for 15 minutes, or until only the center is pink when meatball is broken open.

Remove the pan from the heat. Place the meatballs and spicy sauce on heated serving dish, sprinkle with chopped coriander leaves, and serve immediately.

Shepherd's Pie

4 portions

1 medium-size onion
2 tablespoons plus 1 teaspoon butter
1 tablespoon oil
1½ teaspoons flour
½ cup hot stock

1 cup chopped peeled tomatoes (see Note)
1½ cups ground cooked lamb
1 tablespoon Worcestershire sauce
salt and pepper
4 cups mashed cooked potatoes

Peel and chop the onion. Saute the onion in 2 tablespoons of the butter and the oil over low heat for about 8 minutes, until soft and pale gold. Add the flour and cook, stirring, for about 2 minutes. Off the heat, stir in the stock. Return to heat and bring to a boil. Lower heat and simmer for a minute or two. Drain the tomatoes.

Add the ground lamb, the tomatoes, Worcestershire sauce, and salt and pepper to taste to the sauce, and cook together briefly. Turn the mixture into a baking dish and smooth the surface. Top with the mashed potatoes and

crosshatch the top with the tines of a fork. Dot with remaining butter.

Bake in a preheated 375°F oven for 25 to 30 minutes, until heated through and bubbly. If the potatoes are not as browned as you would like, place under the broiler briefly. *Note:* If using canned tomatoes, the juice can be combined with the stock.

Variations: For a professional look, use a pastry bag and pipe the potatoes decoratively on the top of the dish. If you substitute beef for the lamb, it becomes a "cottage pie."

Ham and Potato Cakes

4 portions

1 cup ground cooked ham
1 cup mashed potatoes
2 tablespoons minced parsley
1½ teaspoons grated onion

¼ teaspoon freshly ground pepper
salt (if necessary)
flour for dredging
2 tablespoons bacon drippings
   or vegetable oil

Combine the ham, potatoes, parsley, onion, pepper, and salt if needed. With dampened hands form the mixture into 4 flat cakes. Dip the cakes into the flour and brush off the excess, so they are very lightly dusted. Heat the bacon drippings or oil in a heavy skillet and sauté the cakes for 3 to 4 minutes on each side, until they are nicely browned.

Meatball Brochettes

4 portions

4 ounces medium-size mushrooms
3 tablespoons oil
1 pound lean beef, ground

3 tablespoons grated
   Parmesan cheese
salt and black pepper
8 cherry tomatoes

Wipe the mushrooms, trim stem ends, and brush lightly with 1 tablespoon of the oil. Combine the beef, cheese, 1 tablespoon oil, and salt and pepper to taste. Mix well and divide into 12 portions. Roll each portion firmly between lightly floured hands to form a ball.

Thread 4 skewers with a tomato and then alternate 3 mushrooms and 3 meatballs; finish with another tomato. Brush skewers with remaining oil. Broil or grill 3 to 4 inches from the heat source for 7 to 8 minutes, turning them every 2 minutes, until well browned.

Turkey Hash

4 portions

3 cups ground cooked turkey
3 cups chopped cooked
   potatoes
3 tablespoons chopped green
   pepper
½ cup minced onion

1 teaspoon salt
freshly ground pepper
¾ cup turkey broth or chicken
   stock
4 poached eggs (optional)

Preheat oven to 350°F. Combine turkey, potatoes, green pepper, onion, salt, and pepper to taste. Toss lightly. Add the broth and mix thoroughly. Place in a greased baking dish, or 4 individual baking dishes, and cover with foil. Bake for 20 minutes. Remove the foil and continue baking for an additional 20 minutes, until lightly browned on top. If desired, serve with poached eggs on top of the hash.

Variation: Chicken can be substituted for the turkey.

Taraba

(Meatballs Enclosed in Spinach Leaves)

4 portions

20 large spinach leaves
1 large onion
2 pounds ground lamb
  salt
1 teaspoon paprika

4 tablespoons butter
8 ounces tomato purée
¼ cup lemon juice
  freshly ground pepper

Bring water to boil in a large saucepan. Wash the spinach leaves and trim heavy stems. Add spinach to boiling water, stir once, and drain immediately. Spread leaves out on a layer of paper towels.

Peel onion and mince. Combine lamb, onion, 1½ teaspoons salt, and paprika. Mix ingredients well and form into 20 balls.

Divide lamb balls among spinach leaves, placing one on each. Wrap spinach leaf around lamb ball, enclosing ball completely. Tie with cotton string or trussing thread to se-cure. Continue making packets until all lamb balls have been covered.

In a large, shallow flameproof casserole, melt butter over medium heat. When the foam has subsided, stir in the tomato purée, lemon juice, and 1½ cups water. Bring to a boil, stirring constantly.

Reduce heat to low, carefully add lamb ball packets to the sauce, and cover casserole. Stirring occasionally, sim-mer for 1½ hours or until lamb balls are cooked through.

Season sauce with salt and pepper to taste. Snip ties on packets and discard. Serve taraba immediately.

Part Three

VEGETABLE AND FRUIT SALADS

"To make this condiment your poet begs
The pounded yellow of two hard-boiled eggs;
Two boiled potatoes, passed through kitchen sieve,
Smoothness and softness to the salad give.
Let onion atoms lurk within the bowl,
And, half-suspected, animate the whole.
Of mordant mustard add a single spoon,
Distrust the condiment that bites so soon;
But deem it not, thou man of herbs, a fault
To add a double quantity of salt; Four times the spoon with oil of
Lucca crown,
And twice with vinegar procur'd from town;
And lastly o'er the flavour'd compound toss
A magic soupçon of anchovy sauce.
Oh, green and glorious! Oh, herbaceous treat!
Twould temt the dying anchorite to eat;
Back to the world he'd turn his fleeting soul,
And plunge his fingers in the salad-bowl!
Serenely full, the epicure would say,
'Fate cannot harm me, I have dined today.' "

(The Reverend Sydney Smith, 1771–1845)

The culinary world of salads extends far beyond the familiar bowl of tossed greens. It includes salads made from cooked vegetables, such as the many versions of potato salad, warm or cold, in a variety of dressings; or bean salads swimming in pungent vinaigrette; or salads made from any number of other vegetables like beets, zucchini, artichokes and even eggplants.

Another type of salad that is long overdue for a revival is the fresh fruit salad. A good selection of lovely fresh fruit is available in markets throughout the year, yet all too often it forms a neglected and uninspired part of the average family diet. But modern nutritional studies have shown that fruits with their high vitamin content and their all-important fiber can make a valuable contribution to our health and well-being, proving the truth in the old proverb that an apple a day keeps the doctor away.

In many European countries fresh fruit is treated with great culinary respect and therefore plays as important a part in menu planning as meat or fish or any other staple, rather than being relegated to the role of a between-meals snack. Fruit can be served as an hors d'oeuvre, as the basis for a light main dish, as a pleasant and refreshing side dish to a roast, and makes for a light, delicious ending to a heavy meal. Fresh fruit can be prepared with little fuss or bother and it goes well with meat, cheese, fish, poultry and game.

Large fruits like pineapples and melons can be hollowed out to make attractive natural bowls in which to serve a fresh fruit salad, and smaller, individual salads can be served to charming effect in hollowed-out apples or halves of grapefruits and oranges.

Many of the world's most memorable salads are made by combining fruits with vegetables and some of these combinations have achieved the status of classics. Perhaps one of the most famous examples is the salad of apples and celery created by Oscar Tschirky in the 1890s when he was the maître d'hôtel at the Waldorf-Astoria hotel in New York City. The walnuts that are usually included in the Waldorf Salad today did not appear until later and were not part of Oscar's original recipe.

Apples appear as an ingredient in many other salads and are often paired with cooked beets to excellent effect.

From Spain and from the Middle East come lovely and refreshing salads based on oranges—all on their own, sprinkled with just a little fragrant cinnamon, or in gorgeous combination with thinly sliced radishes, or onions and parsley. These salads are excellent and very refreshing accompaniments to a rich roast, and the following verse by Jonathan Swift demonstrates that it is a tradition of long standing:

Come, buy my fine Oranges, Sauce for your Veal,
And charming when squeez'd in a Pot of brown Ale.
Well roasted, with Sugar and Wine in a Cup,
They'll make a sweet Bishop when Gentlefolks sup.

(The Bishop refers to a hot drink made with port, oranges and spices.) In Spain there is another salad that combines oranges with cooked potatoes in a wonderfully suave and seductive combination. Another delicious salad is made by combining grapefruit and orange sections with cucumbers and mint. This makes a particularly tasty side dish to a roast leg of lamb.

A rather different salad, from Syria, is a vegetable and bread salad called fattoush—a combination of chopped cucumbers, lettuces, tomatoes, scallions, green peppers and a variety of herbs and spices into which toasted bread is tossed just before serving. Perhaps it was this salad that originated our own custom of adding croutons to a salad for extra taste and texture.

When it comes to making salads that combine fresh fruits with vegetables, the list of possibilities is endless and limited only by the fresh ingredients available to you. So be creative and expand your salad repertoire. Excite the palate and please the eye with your own personal approach to an assortment of colors, textures, tastes.

VEGETABLE AND FRUIT SALADS

Learning how to make the most of health-giving raw fruits and vegetables is time well spent. An imaginative medley of contrasting tastes and textures enhanced by the right dressing is a delight to look at as well as to eat. As a bonus for the time- and budget-conscious cook, salads are quick and easy to prepare and relatively cheap. They are versatile too, and not merely something to cheer up leftover cold meats.

Salads can be served as a separate course at the beginning of a meal, as a side dish to accompany a hot main course, as an integral part of the main dish, or at the end of the meal.

Mixed salads can look striking when decoratively arranged—a pretty table centerpiece and the perfect appetizer to impress your guests and get your party off to a good start.

Simply add slices of cooked meat, flaked fish, chopped hard-cooked eggs (wonderful with fruit), cold cooked rice, nuts, or cheese to turn your salad into a satisfying main-course dish—an excellent way to use small quantities of leftover foods.

Several small bowls, each containing a different one-vegetable salad

Segmenting Oranges and Grapefruits

1 Using a sharp knife, cut off a small slice from the stem end of the fruit so the flesh is just exposed.

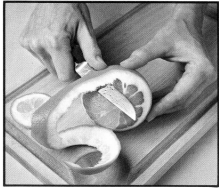

2 Cut away peel in a spiral. Cut sufficiently deep to remove all white inner peel and just a sliver of flesh.

3 Place fruit on a plate or grooved board and cut toward the center to separate a segment.

4 Make a second cut close to the membrane on the other side of the segment and lift out the flesh.

5 Continue in this way until all segments are freed. Extract any seeds with the point of the knife.

6 Squeeze the peel and membranes to extract any juice from remaining slivers of flesh.

Slicing Oranges and Grapefruits

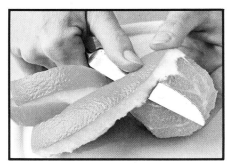

1 Cut away all outer and inner peel as in steps 1 and 2 of segmenting.

2 Keeping the fruit on a plate, cut into ¼-inch-thick slices.

3 Remove seeds with the point of a knife and extract the white core.

Preparing Pineapple

1 Cut away the leafy foliage and take a small slice from the bottom of the pineapple.

2 Cut the pineapple into ½-inch slices, using a sharp serrated knife.

3 Using the point of the knife, remove the woody eyes from the edge of the flesh of each slice.

7 Turn pineapple upside down and carefully lift shell away from flesh, twisting gently to free bottom.

8 Cut the flesh into ½-inch slices, removing eyes and core as shown in steps 3 and 4.

9 For pineapple halves, cut the pineapple, complete with spiky top, into halves.

4 Place in a bowl and pour over any juice left on the cutting plate.

coated with an appropriate dressing, make a handsome addition to a buffet table and enable guests to pick and choose. Several individual salads, plus perhaps a dish of sardines or freshly peeled shrimps, are also ideal to serve as hors d'oeuvres.

Choosing and Storing Salad Vegetables

A salad is as good as its ingredients, and crisp vegetables, such as leafy green ones, lose their freshness easily. Buy little and often and stick to seasonal vegetables: this will insure freshness and help cut housekeeping costs.

Never use size alone as a guide to quality; a large vegetable is not necessarily a good one. In fact, large vegetables tend to be tougher and less delicately flavored. In particular, zucchini, beets, radishes, peas and beans must be young for use in salads.

In general, avoid vegetables that are soft or wilting and those with bruises and a wrinkled or broken skin.

4 Cut away the skin, keeping as close to the flesh as possible. Trim the core and push out.

5 For a whole pineapple, first prepare as 1. Insert a long flexible serrated knife between skin and flesh.

6 Gently move the knife around to free flesh in one piece, but do not cut through the bottom shell.

10 Run a sharp knife around each pineapple half between the shell and the flesh.

11 Lift out the flesh and dice on a plate, removing eyes and woody core.

12 Add chosen extra fruit or flavoring and use to stuff the whole pineapple shell or halves.

Look for firm flesh, glossy skins and crisp leaves.

Most root vegetables store well if kept loose, unwashed and untrimmed, on a ventilated rack in a cold larder or in the bottom of the refrigerator. Soft vegetables that bruise easily need to be carefully wrapped to protect against damage.

Choosing Fruit

When buying fruits to serve raw, always choose the best quality and be sure you select dessert varieties. Over- or underripe or blemished fruits may be cheaper than the prime specimens, but don't forget there is no friendly cooking process or sauce to mask or improve the poor flavor or texture of raw fruit that is not of top quality.

Try always to choose fruit in season. This is when it is most plentiful, at its peak in quality, and cheapest. Wherever possible, buy local fruit. It is usually tastier than fruit shipped in, not having been picked when immature or having suffered the rigors of travel and forced ripening.

Where you buy your fruit has a great effect on the quality you get. If possible, avoid buying fruit in shrink-wrap packs (which can hide a multitude of sins) or buying where there is no one available to give advice. Look for a supermarket that allows customers to examine fruit, buy it by the piece, and ask questions. Or go instead to a local produce market.

Preparing Raw Fruits

All you will need to prepare even the fanciest raw fruit dishes is a sharp knife, preferably of stainless steel with a serrated edge, an apple corer, a grapefruit knife, a citrus juicer, a melon baller, and a citrus zester.

Prepare fruit on a wooden board with a groove to collect the juices, or on a plate. Like vegetables, fruits lose juice and flavor as soon as cut, so it is wise to delay cutting until the last possible moment.

Preparing Melon Baskets

1 *For melon balls*, cut the melon in half and scoop out seeds.

2 If desired give the melon halves a zigzag waterlily edge.

4 Lift out the cutter and shake out the little melon ball.

1 *To make a melon basket*, first cut a thin slice from the base.

4 Make 2 horizontal cuts, stopping when you reach vertical cuts.

5 Lift out the 2 sections of melon and set aside.

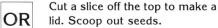
OR Cut a slice off the top to make a lid. Scoop out seeds.

3 Press a melon baller into the flesh and turn in a circle.

2 Make a vertical cut slightly right of the stem to halfway down.

3 Make a parallel cut slightly left of the stem.

6 Cut away flesh from under handle. Remove melon seeds.

7 Cut all the melon flesh into balls and return to the basket.

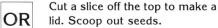

55

Apples, pears and bananas oxidize and begin to turn brown the instant they are cut. To prevent this, rub the fruit with the cut surface of a lemon, dip into lemon juice, or immerse immediately in prepared syrup.

It is often convenient to prepare larger fruits in the kitchen, to save the diners trouble at table, or to add to the appearance of the dish.

Melons. Large melons, such as honeydew and watermelon, which can be served as a first course as well as for dessert, are cut into wedges and seeds are removed with a spoon. A fork is easier for removing watermelon seeds because they are scattered throughout the fruit. Spearing the flesh with a fork, run a knife between the rind and the flesh, and then cut downward to give bite-size chunks that are eaten with a knife and fork. Small cantaloupes are divided into 2 portions, halved across and seeded, then eaten with a spoon. The Italians often serve quarters of lemon with melon so that guests can squeeze the juice over the fruit; this is an excellent way to help bring out the flavor of a slightly underripe or tasteless melon.

Fruit with shells. Oranges, grapefruits, pineapples and melons have firm and attractive skins — natural packaging that can also be used as a serving dish for a fruit salad. Large, very firm bananas can also be used in the same way. Cut the fruit open and scoop out the flesh. Do this carefully, extracting as much flesh as possible but making sure you do not puncture the skin, or the final dish will leak. Cut the flesh into dice, balls, segments or slices, removing inedible parts, then return the cut fruit, alone or mixed with other ingredients, and serve it in the shell. The shell can be made more decorative by cutting it into a basket or waterlily shape if wished. You may be tempted to cut a thin sliver off the bottom of a rounded shell in order to make it stand level, but do not do this, as the fruit juices will leak out at the bottom. Instead, prop it up as discreetly as possible with a crumpled ball of plastic wrap.

Citrus fruits. For really professional looks and best possible eating, oranges and grapefruits should have all their bitter pith and tough membrane removed. Remove seeds also.

Pineapples need to have the woody core and "eyes" embedded in the edge of the flesh removed. Many cooks are afraid of pineapples because they look so unapproachable with all their spines and prickles. They are, however, quite easy to prepare. If yours is a particularly prickly specimen, wear gloves when handling the outer shell.

Apples and pears. Pears are usually nicest peeled, but the color and flavor of apple skin is often a useful addition to dishes, so to peel or not to peel is a matter of personal taste. Cut into rings, quarters, slices or chunks, depending on the recipe. Remember to remove the stem and core and to protect the flesh against oxidization by using lemon juice.

Keeping Fruits Fresh

Once you get fruits home, they should be stored in a cool, dry, airy place to preserve maximum freshness and flavor.

Refrigeration is best for holding all ripe fruits except bananas. Apples will keep for up to 2 weeks, citrus fruits for 3 weeks and just ripe pears and bananas for 1 week. Ideally, the fruits should be spaced out so they do not touch each other. This will prevent spoilage if one piece of fruit should go bad. Bananas will keep in cool, airy conditions for 1 week.

Melons, pineapples and grapes, wrapped whole, will keep for 3 to 4 days. Cut melons and pineapples should be wrapped in plastic wrap before storing or they will absorb other food flavors, and melons can contribute their own flavor to other foods in the refrigerator.

Vegetable Salad Ideas

What goes with what? One-vegetable salads can be delicious, but a mixture of textures, colors and flavors can be very appetizing too. Some very suc-

cessful mixed salads are described here, or you can have fun creating your own salad recipes. Be careful to choose ingredients that complement each other or you could end up with a hodgepodge of a salad.

As a general rule—though not a fast one—it is best to add any dressing just before serving; this is especially important for vegetables—such as lettuce, sliced tomatoes or cucumbers—that wilt or lose texture easily. Some harder vegetables, such as peas, beans, cauliflower, celery, fennel and mushrooms, benefit from being dressed before they are served. This often softens them slightly and gives their flavors a chance to penetrate. You will need about 1/2 cup of dressing for a large salad serving 4 portions.

• Cauliflower makes an excellent base for a winter salad. Mix flowerets with a little grated carrot, parsnip or celeriac. Add plenty of unpeeled sliced green apple and coat with lemon-flavored vinaigrette.

• To make a main-course dish to follow a hearty soup, add cubes of cold pork or ham and a handful of peanuts to a cauliflower salad.

• Cut button mushrooms into thin slices, sprinkle with lemon juice, salt and black pepper, and leave for 30 minutes. Then toss in olive oil and mix with seedless white grapes for a delicious first course.

• For a healthy salad, surround a mound of grated carrots with slices of avocado. Top with walnut pieces and watercress sprigs and dress with freshly squeezed orange juice.

• For a salad to serve at the end of a meal with cheese, mix paper-thin slivers of fennel with watercress sprigs. Sprinkle on some olive oil and a little sea salt; top with toasted almonds just before serving.

• Greek salad makes a good appetizer or, served with crusty hot French bread, a summery lunch dish. Mix strips of red pepper, sliced tomatoes and black olives with a little shredded white cabbage and onion rings. Dress with a garlicky vinaigrette to which several lightly crushed coriander seeds have been added. Top the salad with a

scattering of cubed feta cheese or white Stilton.

• Sprinkle a little chopped fresh basil on thin-sliced tomatoes and serve as part of an hors d'oeuvre or as a side salad.

• For a dinner party first course or a cool lunch dish, combine balls of avocado and melon with peeled shrimps or bite-size pieces of cooked chicken. Toss in freshly squeezed lemon juice and add a scattering of cashew nuts and chopped fresh mint just before serving.

• Make a tasty and attractive appetizer by halving and pitting an avocado. Fill the cavities with grated celeriac moistened with sour-cream dressing. Top with the feathery fronds of fennel or sprigs of mint. Allow 1 avocado per person and serve with whole-wheat rolls for a nutritious meal.

• Make an unusual and refreshing Oriental salad by mixing bean sprouts with a few scallions and chopped celery. Topped with a layer of sliced snow peas, tomatoes and watercress, this looks beautiful too. Use green peppers, sliced orange and fronds of feathery fennel to make an excellent and attractive alternative topping for this salad.

• Marinate tiny button mushrooms in vinaigrette and drain; add peanuts and watercress to make an excellent side salad to accompany roast chicken or duck.

• Make an exotic Middle East salad with strips of pepper, minced onion, quarters of tomato and a few crushed coriander seeds. Moisten with a little freshly squeezed lemon juice and serve with tahini dressing and warmed pita bread.

Savory Fruit Salads

Savory fruit salads are excellent fare for first courses, light lunches, suppers or as a refresher between the main dish and the dessert in a hearty meal.

Those containing meat are well suited to dieters as a main course because they are satisfying without being fattening. They are also useful for packed lunches because the fruit does not become limp when dressed.

Salade Niçoise

6 portions

12 ounces fresh green beans
1 pound waxy new potatoes
10 large plum tomatoes
6 anchovy fillets
10 ounces canned tuna,
    oil-packed or
    water-packed
12 oil-cured black olives
¾ cup Vinaigrette Dressing
    (see Index)
1 tablespoon minced fresh
    parsley
1 tablespoon minced fresh
    basil

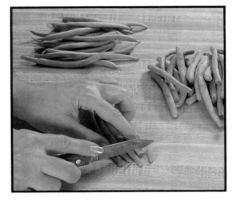

1 Wash and trim green beans; leave them whole. Cook in boiling salted water until crisp-tender, not mushy.

2 Scrub potatoes and cook in boiling water until tender. Cool, peel, and chop potatoes.

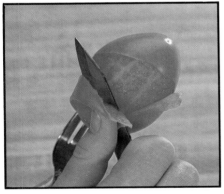

3 Blanch and peel tomatoes. Cut 6 into thick slices and chop the rest. Remove as many seeds as possible.

4 Cut anchovy fillets into halves. Drain and flake the tuna.

5 Combine chopped potatoes and tomatoes in the center of a large serving platter. Place tuna on top.

6 Divide beans into 6 bundles and arrange around the tuna. Place sliced tomatoes around the edge of the dish.

7 Top tomatoes with anchovy pieces and olives, arranged alternately.

8 Spoon dressing over the salad and sprinkle everything with minced parsley and basil.

Pepper and Yogurt Salad

4 portions

1 large green bell pepper
1 large red bell pepper
1 large yellow bell pepper
8 large leaves of leaf lettuce
½ cup plain yogurt
1 tablespoon lemon juice
  salt and black pepper
  ground ginger

1 Char the peppers under the broiler until skins are blackened. When peppers are cool, peel them.

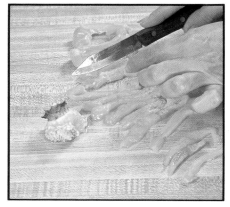

2 Discard stems, seeds and ribs. Cut peppers from top to bottom into thin lengthwise strips.

3 Wash, dry, and shred the lettuce. Divide lettuce evenly among 4 individual salad plates.

4 Beat yogurt and lemon juice together and season with salt, pepper and ginger to taste.

5 Add pepper strips to yogurt and mix gently. Spoon pepper and yogurt mixture on the lettuce, dividing it evenly.

Savory fruit salads are usually a combination of fruits, vegetables, fish or meat in a dressing. This can be a good egg-based mayonnaise, a vinaigrette or a number of other types of dressings.

When making vinaigrette for savory fruit salads, use fruit juice instead of vinegar. Lemon, lime, pineapple, grapefruit and orange juice are all good. Failing this, cider or tarragon vinegar can be used. Blue cheese and mustard vinaigrettes also go well with fruit.

• For a packed lunch salad, arrange slices of apple (dipped into lemon juice to prevent browning), orange segments and drained tuna fish on a shell of crisp lettuce leaves.
• For a refresher salad, peel a lemon and chop it into tiny pieces. Mix with crisp lettuce or curly chicory, cucumber, scallions and lots of chopped fresh parsley. Dress with a plain vinaigrette.
• For a refreshing and unusual hors d'oeuvre, serve sliced pears on a bed of Chinese cabbage. Dress with bluecheese vinaigrette.

• For a main-course salad, mix pineapple cubes or melon balls with ham, cold chicken, cold lamb or cold roast beef, cubed cheese and grapes.
• For an Italian hors d'oeuvre, serve melon quarters or pear halves on a bed of thin slices of prosciutto. If you are unable to obtain prosciutto, use baked ham cut into thin slivers.
• For a tasty accompaniment to cold ham, serve pineapple cubes on a bed of crisp endive. Dress with a pineapple vinaigrette and sprinkle with chopped fresh parsley.

Sour-Cream Dressing

*This is excellent with grated root vegetables such as
celeriac and carrot, particularly if you garnish it with
chopped fresh mint, dill or fennel.*

½ cup, enough for 4 portions

1 small garlic clove
   juice of 1 lemon
1 teaspoon sugar
   pinch of salt

   freshly ground pepper
½ cup sour cream
1 to 2 tablespoons minced
   fresh herbs

Crush the garlic clove in a small bowl. Mix in the lemon juice, sugar, salt and pepper to taste. Stir in the sour cream and fresh herbs. Use parsley, chervil, chives, mint, basil, or a combination of several herbs.

Spicy Tomato Dressing

*This dressing is easy to make and particularly good with
salads made from cauliflower and zucchini.*

⅔ cup, enough for 4 to 6 portions

4 tablespoons ketchup
4 tablespoons olive oil
2 tablespoons light cream

   dash of chili sauce
   salt and freshly ground pepper
   sugar

Put the ketchup, olive oil, cream and chili sauce into a glass jar with a screw-top lid. Screw lid firmly and shake the jar vigorously until all the ingredients are well blended. Season with salt, freshly ground black pepper and sugar to taste.

Vinaigrette Dressing

½ cup, enough for 4 portions

1 garlic clove
2 tablespoons wine vinegar
6 tablespoons olive oil
¼ teaspoon salt
⅛ teaspoon black pepper

½ teaspoon prepared
   Dijon-style mustard
1 teaspoon minced fresh dill
1 teaspoon minced fresh
   parsley

Peel garlic and put through a press into a screw-top jar. Add all other dressing ingredients and shake vigorously until well mixed. If not using immediately, be sure to shake the dressing again before serving.

Bittersweet Dressing

*This dressing is excellent with a grated carrot salad or
coleslaw. The sweetness of the marmalade is offset by
the sharpness of the lemon juice and scallions.*

1 cup, enough for 6 portions

8 ounces cottage cheese
2 tablespoons orange
   marmalade
2 tablespoons buttermilk

3 tablespoons freshly squeezed
   lemon juice
2 scallions

Push the cottage cheese through a fine sieve, using the back of a wooden spoon, to remove any lumps. Add the marmalade and mix well. Stir in the buttermilk, then the lemon juice. Mince the scallions and stir them into the dressing.

Green Bean Salad

4 portions

1 pound fresh green snap beans	½ cup Vinaigrette Dressing (see Index)
½ teaspoon salt	

Wash the beans, top and tail them, but leave whole. Pour 6 cups water into a saucepan and bring to a boil over high heat. Add the salt and beans and return water to the boil. Reduce heat to moderate and cook the beans for 5 to 15 minutes, until tender but still somewhat crisp. Drain beans in a colander, immediately pour cold water over them, and drain again. Transfer beans to a large bowl. Pour dressing over the beans and mix gently to coat thoroughly. Chill salad in the refrigerator before serving.

Cauliflower Salad

4 portions

1 medium-size cauliflower	1 teaspoon sugar
salt	1 teaspoon freshly ground
½ cup chopped walnuts	black pepper
6 tablespoons olive oil	1 tablespoon minced fresh
2 tablespoons white-wine vinegar	parsley
1 teaspoon lemon juice	2 tablespoons crumbled
½ teaspoon prepared Dijon-style mustard	Roquefort cheese

Wash cauliflower, break it into florets, and soak them in cold salted water for 10 minutes. Drain, then chop into bite-size pieces. Discard the base and hard ends of the stems. Put cauliflower into a large salad bowl and add the chopped walnuts.

Make a dressing by combining the oil, vinegar, lemon juice, mustard, sugar, pepper and 1 teaspoon salt in a screw-top jar. Shake the jar vigorously to blend all ingredients well. Add the parsley and crumbled Roquefort and shake again. Pour the dressing over the cauliflower and walnuts and toss to mix thoroughly. Chill the salad in the refrigerator for 30 minutes before serving.

Rumanian Marinated Pepper Salad

4 portions

- 4 green peppers
- 4 red peppers
- 6 tablespoons distilled white vinegar
- 2 tablespoons medium-dry sherry
- 1 tablespoon Worcestershire sauce
- 6 tablespoons olive oil
- 1 teaspoon salt
  freshly ground black pepper
- 2 teaspoons sugar
- 1 teaspoon paprika
- 8 ounces cream cheese, cold
- 12 pitted black olives

Wash and dry the peppers. Halve them, and discard stems, seeds and ribs. Cut the peppers into quarters. Half-fill a saucepan with water and bring to a boil. Add peppers and blanch for 3 minutes. Drain and dry on paper towels. Cool.

Pour the vinegar, sherry, Worcestershire sauce and oil into a mixing bowl. Add the salt, 8 grindings of pepper, the sugar and paprika. Stir well to mix. Taste and add more seasoning if necessary. Put the peppers into the marinade and turn and mix to coat them with the mixture. Cover and marinate in the refrigerator for 24 hours.

At serving time, lift peppers from the liquid and arrange in a shallow bowl or serving dish. Spoon a little marinade over them, enough to moisten the tops. Cut the cold cream cheese into cubes and sprinkle cheese cubes and the olives over the peppers. Serve at once.

Chicory, Fennel and Tomato Salad

4 to 6 portions

- 1 fennel bulb
- 1 head of chicory
- 4 tomatoes
- 4 tablespoons olive oil
- 2 tablespoons white-wine vinegar
- ½ teaspoon salt
- ¼ teaspoon black pepper
- 1 garlic clove

Wash and trim fennel; cut the bulb into thin slices. Wash chicory and discard any coarse or damaged outer leaves. Separate the head into leaves; cut large leaves into 2 or 3 pieces. Wash tomatoes and cut into thin slices. Place vegetables in a serving dish.

Combine the oil, vinegar, salt and pepper in a screw-top jar. Peel garlic and put through a press into the dressing. Shake well. Pour dressing over the vegetables and toss well. Chill the salad for 30 minutes before serving.

Eastern European Potato Salad

8 portions

2 pounds potatoes	1 teaspoon dried dill
1 teaspoon salt	1 tablespoon chopped fresh
1 large dill pickle	parsley
1 small onion	1½ cups mayonnaise

Scrub and peel the potatoes and place in a large saucepan. Cover with water and add the salt. Cook over moderately high heat for 15 to 20 minutes, until potatoes are tender but still firm. Drain. Cut potatoes into small cubes or strips and put them in a large salad bowl. Mince the pickle; peel and mince the onion. Add pickle, onion, dill and parsley to the potatoes and mix well. Pour in the mayonnaise; using 2 large spoons, toss carefully to coat potatoes. Serve at once or let cool to room temperature, tossing occasionally, if you prefer to serve it cold.

Potato, Cheese and Prosciutto Salad

4 portions

1 pound waxy new potatoes	1 garlic clove
3 ounces Gruyère cheese	½ cup mayonnaise
2 ounces Gorgonzola cheese	½ teaspoon black pepper
4 slices of prosciutto, about 6 ounces	⅛ teaspoon cayenne pepper

Scrub potatoes and cook in boiling water until tender. Drain. Cool and peel potatoes, then place on a board and cut into ½-inch cubes. Transfer potatoes to a mixing bowl. Cut Gruyère cheese into ¼-inch cubes. Crumble the Gorgonzola. Cut the slices of prosciutto into halves and roll up each half-slice. Peel garlic and put through a press into the potatoes. Add the mayonnaise, black pepper, cayenne, and both cheeses to the bowl of potatoes and toss with 2 large spoons until ingredients are well mixed.

Transfer the salad to a glass salad bowl. Garnish with the rolled prosciutto and serve immediately.

Fontina-Cheese and Red-Pepper Salad

4 portions

3 large red peppers
8 ounces fontina cheese

6 cooked artichoke hearts
8 small anchovy fillets

Mustard Dressing

3 tablespoons olive oil
1 tablespoon white-wine vinegar
1 teaspoon prepared
    Dijon-style mustard

½ teaspoon salt
¼ teaspoon black pepper
½ teaspoon sugar

Wash and halve peppers, discard stems, seeds and ribs, and cut peppers from stem to blossom end into thin strips. Cut the cheese into ½-inch cubes. Halve the artichoke hearts.

Combine peppers, cheese and artichoke hearts in a salad bowl. Lay anchovy fillets on top.

Combine dressing ingredients in a cup or small bowl. Blend and pour dressing over the salad. Toss at the table.

Italian Mushroom and Green-Pea Salad

4 portions

8 ounces button mushrooms
3 tablespoons olive oil
1 tablespoon fresh lemon juice
¼ teaspoon salt

⅛ teaspoon black pepper
¾ cup cooked peas
1 head of Boston lettuce

Wipe mushrooms with a damp cloth, trim base of stems, and cut mushrooms into thin slices.

Combine the oil, lemon juice, salt and pepper in a screw-top jar and shake well. Place mushroom slices and peas in a mixing bowl and pour the dressing over them. Toss well. Chill the salad in the refrigerator for 30 minutes.

Wash lettuce, discard outer leaves, and shred lettuce. Line a serving dish with the shredded lettuce. Remove salad from refrigerator and pile it in the center of the lettuce. Serve at once.

Fattoush

(Syrian Vegetable and Bread Salad)

This peasant dish combines many flavors and introduces an unusual texture with the toasted bread or pita.

Fattoush may be prepared in advance and chilled. Do not stir in the toasted bread until just before serving.

4 portions

1 large cucumber
5 tomatoes
1 small head of lettuce
10 scallions
1 small green pepper
1 garlic clove
1 tablespoon minced fresh
    coriander leaves

1 tablespoon minced fresh parsley
1½ teaspoons minced fresh mint
6 tablespoons olive oil
    juice of 2 lemons
½ teaspoon salt
¼ teaspoon black pepper
5 thin slices of bread, or 2 pita
    breads

Peel and chop cucumber and tomatoes. Shred the lettuce. Trim and chop scallions. Halve pepper, discard stem, seeds and ribs, and chop pepper. Peel garlic and put through a press. Place cucumber and tomatoes in a salad bowl. Add the lettuce, scallions, green pepper, garlic, coriander, parsley and mint.

Pour the olive oil and lemon juice over the vegetables and sprinkle in the salt and pepper. Toss the salad so all ingredients are well coated with oil and lemon juice.

Toast the bread, or split and toast the pitas, and cut into small cubes. Stir the toasted bread cubes into the salad and serve at once.

Rice Salad with Cheese, Walnuts and Artichokes

6 to 8 portions

6 scallions	¾ cup Vinaigrette Dressing (see Index)
4 ounces fresh spinach	4 tablespoons mayonnaise
6 ounces Gruyère cheese	2 tablespoons dairy sour cream
⅔ cup shelled walnuts	½ teaspoon salt
4 cooked large artichoke hearts	½ teaspoon white pepper
4 cups cooked long-grain rice	¾ teaspoon cayenne pepper

Wash and trim scallions and mince them. Wash spinach thoroughly, shake dry, and chop, or cut into small pieces with kitchen scissors. Cut cheese into cubes. Chop the walnuts. Cool the artichoke hearts; cut 2 hearts into small dice and cut the rest into thick slices.

Place the cooked rice and minced scallions in a large bowl and pour the vinaigrette dressing over them. Toss the rice mixture until well coated with dressing. Transfer the mixture to a large serving dish.

In a second mixing bowl, combine the spinach, Gruyère cheese, walnuts and diced artichokes. Combine the mayonnaise, sour cream, salt, white pepper and cayenne, and beat to blend well. Spoon the cheese and walnut mixture over the rice bed. Arrange the sliced artichokes decoratively around the sides of the serving dish. Chill the salad in the refrigerator for 30 minutes before serving.

Arabian Oranges

4 portions

6 large oranges	1 cup dry white wine
4 ounces fresh dates	4 ounces slivered blanched almonds

Cut 4 oranges into segments, removing all white inner peel, membranes and pits. Place orange slices in a bowl. Cut dates into halves, remove pits, and cut fruit into slivers with kitchen scissors. Add dates to the oranges.

Squeeze juice from remaining oranges and mix with the wine. Pour the liquid over the fruits. Cover and chill for at least 4 hours, turning the mixture occasionally. Scatter the almonds over the fruits just before serving.

Cauliflower and Green Beans à la Grecque

6 portions

1	small cauliflower		12	coriander seeds
1	pound fresh green beans		1	garlic clove
1	Spanish onion		8	ounces tomatoes
6	tablespoons olive oil			salt
½	cup dry white wine		½	lemon
	freshly ground black pepper		12	pitted black olives
1	bouquet garni (see Volume 1 Index)		2	tablespoons chopped parsley

Rinse the cauliflower and break into florets. Wash the beans and top and tail them. Beans may be left whole or halved crosswise. Peel and mince the onion. Heat 2 tablespoons of the oil in a deep heavy pan and sauté the onion for about 5 minutes. Remove pan from heat. Add the wine, black pepper to taste, the *bouquet garni* and the coriander seeds. Peel and crush the garlic and add to the pan.

Peel the tomatoes, chop them, and remove as many seeds as possible. Add tomatoes, cauliflower and beans to the pan. Mix well. Bring liquid to a boil and season to taste with salt. Cook over moderate heat for 10 minutes, stirring occasionally. The sauce should be reduced, but if it evaporates too fast, add a little water.

When the cooking time is up, remove pan from heat and discard the *bouquet garni.* Leave the vegetables in the liquid to cool.

When the mixture is cold, stir in remaining olive oil. Squeeze the lemon and add the juice, and extra seasoning if needed. Arrange the cauliflower and beans in a serving dish with the sauce. Dot with the olives and sprinkle with parsley. Chill until ready to serve.

Garlic Salad

4 portions

6 large lettuce leaves
8 hard-cooked eggs
4 medium-size tomatoes

1 small green pepper
8 anchovy fillets

Garlic Dressing

3 garlic cloves
1 tablespoon minced fresh
   parsley
¼ teaspoon dry mustard
¼ teaspoon salt

¼ teaspoon freshly ground
   black pepper
4 tablespoons olive oil
1 tablespoon tarragon vinegar
1 tablespoon lemon juice

Wash lettuce leaves and shake dry. Peel and slice eggs. Wash and slice tomatoes. (They may be peeled if you prefer.) Wash and halve the pepper, discard stem, seeds and ribs, and chop the pepper. Arrange the lettuce leaves on a large serving platter. Place egg and tomato slices on the lettuce, in alternating layers, beginning from the center of the dish.

Sprinkle on the chopped green pepper. Roll up the anchovy fillets and arrange them on the outer edge of the dish.

Make the dressing: Peel garlic cloves and put through a press into a bowl. Add the parsley, mustard, salt and pepper. Slowly beat in the oil, vinegar and lemon juice. Combine the mixture thoroughly and pour it over the salad. Chill the salad in the refrigerator for 15 minutes before serving.

Hungarian Apple Salad

4 portions

4 medium-size potatoes, about
   1 pound
1 small onion
2 large red-skinned eating
   apples
1 tablespoon seedless raisins
¼ cup olive oil

2 tablespoons white-wine
   vinegar
1 teaspoon lemon juice
½ teaspoon salt
¼ teaspoon black pepper
1 tablespoon snipped fresh
   chives

Scrub and cook the potatoes; cool, peel, and chop them. Peel onion and cut into thin slices; separate slices into rings. Wash and core apples; do not peel them; dice them. Combine chopped potatoes, onion rings, diced apples and raisins in a salad bowl.

Combine remaining ingredients to make a dressing; beat with a fork until well blended. Pour dressing over the vegetables and fruits and toss well. Chill the salad in the refrigerator for 30 minutes before serving with cold meats or fish.

Apple Walnut Salad with Cream-Cheese Dressing

4 portions

4 red-skinned eating apples
  juice of 1 lemon
2 celery ribs
16 black grapes
	½ cup shelled walnuts
	4 ounces cream cheese
	2 tablespoons milk
	  salt and black pepper

Core the apples and cut into quarters, then into slices. Immediately dip slices into lemon juice. Place apple slices in a bowl. Wash and dry celery; chop it, and add to the apples. Halve the grapes, remove seeds, and add grapes to the bowl. Chop the walnuts, reserving a few for decoration, and add nuts to the bowl.

Place the cream cheese in a separate small bowl. Add

the milk and beat until smooth. Season to taste. Spoon the dressing on the apple mixture; mix well. Sprinkle remaining walnuts on top.

Variations: For a pleasant alternative to celery, use grated celeriac or carrot. Hazelnuts can be used in place of walnuts.

Potato Salad

4 portions

1 pound waxy new potatoes
½ cup mayonnaise
1 tablespoon lemon juice
1 tablespoon olive oil
½ teaspoon salt
	½ teaspoon black pepper
	2 tablespoons snipped fresh
	  chives
	4 tablespoons chopped
	  scallions

Scrub potatoes and cook in boiling water until tender. Drain. Cool, peel, and slice potatoes. Place three quarters of the potatoes in a mixing bowl. Spoon the mayonnaise over them and sprinkle with the lemon juice, oil, salt, pepper and 1 tablespoon of the chives. Using 2 large spoons, carefully toss the potatoes until they are thoroughly coated with the dressing. Spoon the salad into a serving bowl.

Arrange remaining potato slices over the top of the salad. Sprinkle with remaining chives and scatter the scallions around the edge of the bowl. Cover the bowl and chill in the refrigerator for 30 minutes before serving; or, if you prefer, serve the salad at room temperature.

Zucchini Salad

4 portions

1 pound small zucchini
1 large orange
4 ounces fresh green beans
1 large carrot
4 ounces button mushrooms
	4 medium-size tomatoes
	2 tablespoons minced fresh
	  mint
	½ cup Vinaigrette Dressing (see
	  Index)

Scrub and scrape zucchini, cut them into chunks, and steam until crisp-tender. Cool and dice. Peel orange, remove all white inner peel, cut into segments, and halve the segments; remove all the pits. Wash and trim beans, blanch until crisp-tender, rinse with cold water, and cool. Cut each bean crosswise into halves. Scrape and dice the carrot. Wipe mush-

rooms with a damp cloth, trim base of stems, and slice both caps and stems. Wash tomatoes and cut into thin slices.

Place all these ingredients in a salad bowl and mix gently. Stir 1 tablespoon of the minced mint into the dressing and pour dressing over the salad. Toss well. Sprinkle remaining mint over the salad and serve immediately.

68

Tomato and Mozzarella Salad

6 portions

6 large tomatoes
1 pound mozzarella cheese
12 anchovy fillets
36 pitted black olives
1 teaspoon salt

½ teaspoon black pepper
1 teaspoon sugar
1 tablespoon minced fresh basil
4 tablespoons olive oil
1 tablespoon wine vinegar

Blanch and peel tomatoes and cut them into ¼-inch-thick slices. Cut the cheese into slices of the same thickness. Place 1 slice of tomato in the center of an individual plate. Surround with remaining slices of 1 tomato. Place 1 slice of mozzarella on the tomato in the center and arrange 4 more cheese slices over the surrounding tomatoes. Arrange 2 anchovy fillets in a cross over the central slice of cheese.

Scatter 6 olives over the salad. Arrange remaining ingredients in the same way, on 5 other plates.

Combine the salt, pepper, sugar and basil in a small bowl. Beat in the oil and vinegar, a little at a time, until the dressing is combined. Pour dressing over the salads just before serving them, as a salad or a first course.

Potato Salad with Herbs

4 portions

1 pound waxy new potatoes
8 scallions
1 tablespoon minced fresh parsley
2 teaspoons minced fresh basil
1 teaspoon minced fresh marjoram
½ teaspoon minced fresh lemon thyme

½ teaspoon snipped fresh fennel leaves
6 tablespoons olive oil
2 tablespoons wine vinegar
1 teaspoon salt
½ teaspoon black pepper
½ teaspoon sugar

Scrub potatoes and cook in boiling water until tender. Drain. Cool and peel them, then cut into ½-inch cubes. Place potatoes in a serving bowl. Trim and chop scallions. Add scallions and all the herbs to the potatoes.

Combine the olive oil, vinegar, salt, pepper and sugar in a small mixing bowl. Beat with a fork until the dressing is well mixed. Pour dressing over the potatoes and herbs and serve immediately; or chill in the refrigerator before serving.

Dutch Vegetable Salad

4 portions

Cooked Asparagus Dressing

2 tablespoons butter
2 tablespoons flour
¾ cup milk
2 tablespoons cider vinegar
6 tablespoons light cream
¼ teaspoon salt
¼ teaspoon white pepper
1 teaspoon grated lemon rind
1 teaspoon snipped fresh chives
½ teaspoon dried chervil
8 ounces cooked asparagus

3 medium-size carrots
1 small turnip
1 small onion
1 green pepper
1 small cucumber
4 celery ribs
4 ounces button mushrooms
8 small scallions
1 teaspoon paprika

First make the dressing. Melt the butter in a small saucepan over moderate heat. Remove pan from heat. With a wooden spoon stir in the flour to make a smooth paste. Gradually add the milk, stirring constantly. Return pan to heat and cook, still stirring, for 2 to 3 minutes, until the sauce is thick and smooth. Add the vinegar and continue to cook and stir for 2 minutes longer. Again remove pan from heat and add the cream, salt, pepper, lemon rind, chives and chervil; mix until ingredients are thoroughly combined. Dampen a circle of wax paper large enough to cover the sauce and press it on the surface of the sauce to keep out air. Set sauce aside to cool completely.

Purée the cooked asparagus through a food mill or in a food processor. Force the purée through a strainer into a bowl; discard the fibers in the strainer. Discard the paper on the surface of the sauce. When the sauce is cool, add the asparagus purée and beat well.

Scrub and scrape the carrots. Peel the turnip and onion. Wash and halve the pepper, and discard stem, seeds and ribs. Grate carrots, turnip, onion and pepper by hand or in a food processor fitted with the steel blade or a fine shredding disk. Wash cucumber, or peel it if it has been waxed, and halve lengthwise. Remove seeds and chop the cucumber. Wash and dry celery, trim, and cut into 2-inch strips. Wipe mushrooms with a damp cloth, discard stems, and cut caps into thin slices. Wash and trim scallions, quarter them lengthwise, and cut the lengths into 2-inch pieces. Combine all these vegetables in a large mixing bowl.

Pour the asparagus dressing over the vegetables. Toss the mixture until vegetables are well coated with the sauce. Spoon the salad into a glass bowl and sprinkle with paprika. Either serve at once, or chill until required.

Kumquat and Pineapple Salad

4 portions

8 ounces preserved kumquats
8 ounces fresh pineapple
4 ounces green grapes
6 large lettuce leaves
1¼ cups dairy sour cream

½ teaspoon dried tarragon
1 tablespoon lemon juice
½ teaspoon salt
¼ teaspoon white pepper

Cut the kumquats into crosswise slices and remove the seeds. Peel, core, and chop pineapple. Wash and dry grapes, halve them, and remove any seeds. Wash and dry lettuce leaves.

Make a dressing by combining sour cream, tarragon, lemon juice and seasonings. Beat with a fork until well blended. Add the kumquats, pineapple and grapes to the dressing and mix well.

Arrange lettuce leaves on a large serving plate. Spoon the salad onto the lettuce. Chill the salad in the refrigerator for 30 minutes before serving.
Note: If preserved kumquats are not available, substitute 8 ounces of orange segments and 1 teaspoon of preserved stem ginger, minced.

Watercress, Fennel, Cucumber and Tomato Salad

4 portions

1 bunch of watercress	1 scallion
½ fennel bulb	2 tablespoons chopped pimiento
½ small cucumber	
4 tomatoes	½ cup Vinaigrette Dressing (see Index)
6 anchovy fillets	

Wash watercress, shake dry, and remove all thick stems. Divide watercress into small sprigs. Wash and trim fennel and cut into thin slices. Peel and slice cucumber. Wash and core tomatoes and cut into quarters. Cut each anchovy fillet into 2 pieces. Wash and trim scallion, and mince it. Combine all these ingredients and the pimiento in a large bowl and toss with 2 spoons until well mixed.

Pour the dressing into the mixture and toss gently until all ingredients are well coated with dressing. Serve at once.

Beet and Apple Salad

4 portions

3 medium-size raw beets
3 medium-size cooking apples
⅓ cup golden raisins
1 tablespoon prepared
      horseradish sauce
4 tablespoons vegetable oil

2 tablespoons wine vinegar
1 teaspoon sugar
½ teaspoon salt
½ teaspoon freshly ground
      black pepper

Peel the beets and coarsely grate them into a salad bowl. Core the apples. Coarsely grate them and add to the beets. Mix in the raisins.

Make the dressing by mixing all remaining ingredients in a small bowl. Pour the dressing over the salad, toss lightly, and serve.

Munkaczina

(Orange and Olive Salad)

4 portions

2 large oranges
1 Spanish onion
20 pitted black olives

pinch of red pepper
coarse salt
3 tablespoons walnut or olive oil

Peel the oranges completely, removing all the white inner peel. Slice the oranges; remove seeds and the white portion in the center. Lay the oranges in a serving bowl. Peel the onion, cut into thin slices, and push slices into rings. Sprinkle onion rings over the orange slices and scatter the olives on top. Add a seasoning of red pepper, a sprinkling of coarse salt, and pour the oil over all. Cover the salad and chill for 1 hour before serving to allow the flavors to blend.

Italian Orange and Tomato Salad

4 portions

1 head of lettuce
2 oranges
1 large tomato
   juice of ½ lemon

1 tablespoon vegetable oil
1 teaspoon snipped fresh chives
½ teaspoon salt
¼ teaspoon white pepper

Remove outer lettuce leaves, wash lettuce, and shred it. Place lettuce on a flat serving dish. Peel oranges completely and separate into segments. Remove any seeds. Blanch and peel the tomato and cut into thin slices. Place orange segments and tomato slices in a mixing bowl.

Combine remaining ingredients in a screw-top jar to make a dressing. Shake well to blend, then pour over the fruits and toss gently to blend. Arrange the mixture on the lettuce and chill in the refrigerator for 15 minutes before serving.

Pear Salad with Brie Cheese

8 portions

4 medium-size firm pears
   juice of ½ lemon
4 ounces ripe Brie cheese

3 tablespoons dry white wine
½ cup walnut halves
1 bunch of watercress

Cut the pears lengthwise into halves. Core them and peel, removing the thinnest possible layer of pear under the peel. Brush the pears with lemon juice and place 1 pear half on each plate.

Mash the Brie with a fork and blend in the wine. When the mixture is smooth and creamy, stir in all but 8 walnut halves. Pile the mixture on top of the pears. Top each one with a walnut half and surround with watercress sprigs.

Deviled Oranges

4 portions

1 large onion	4 tablespoons sliced stuffed green olives
4 oranges	1 tablespoon minced fresh parsley
¼ cup olive oil	
¼ teaspoon cayenne pepper	

Peel and slice the onion and separate slices into rings. Peel oranges and cut into crosswise slices. Heat the oil in a large heavy frying pan over moderate heat. Add the onion rings and cook them for 5 minutes on each side, until they are almost soft but not browned. With a slotted spoon remove onion rings from the pan and drain them on paper towels.

Put the orange slices in one layer in a shallow serving dish. Arrange onion rings on top and sprinkle with cayenne pepper and sliced olives. Sprinkle the minced parsley over all and serve immediately.

Grapefruit and Avocado Salad

4 portions

1 large grapefruit	2 teaspoons sugar
2 heads of Belgian endive	3 tablespoons Vinaigrette Dressing (see Index)
2 large ripe avocados	
2 teaspoons lemon juice	

Peel grapefruit completely and chop the segments. Wash and trim the endives and cut across into thin slices. Halve the avocados and remove pits. Using a teaspoon, scoop out the avocado pulp and place it in a mixing bowl. Reserve the avocado shells. Add 1 teaspoon of the lemon juice, the chopped grapefruit and sliced endive to the avocados. Sprinkle in the sugar. Using a silver or stainless-steel fork, mash the ingredients until they form a relatively smooth mixture. Stir the dressing into the avocado mixture, then spoon the mixture into the reserved avocado shells. Sprinkle remaining lemon juice over the filling. Cover with wax paper or foil. Chill the filled avocados in the refrigerator for at least 30 minutes. Serve cold.

Grapefruit and Orange Salad

4 portions

2 medium-size grapefruits	½ teaspoon lemon juice
1 large orange	1 teaspoon sugar
½ cucumber	½ teaspoon black pepper
fresh mint leaves	½ teaspoon salt
3 tablespoons corn oil	

Peel grapefruits and orange completely. With a sharp knife, separate both into segments, removing all the white inner peel, the membranes and any pits. Place fruits in a shallow salad bowl. Halve the cucumber lengthwise, remove any hard seeds, then cut the cucumber into ¼-inch crosswise slices. Arrange cucumber slices decoratively around the fruit mixture. Wash and dry mint leaves.

Combine remaining ingredients to make a dressing and beat with a fork until well blended. Pour the dressing over the salad and decorate with the mint leaves. Chill the salad in the refrigerator for at least 30 minutes before serving with glazed ham or roast lamb.

Part Four

SPONGECAKES AND GÉNOISES

"Pat-a-cake, pat-a-cake, baker's man
Bake me a cake as fast as you can."

—Nursery Rhyme

We bake a cake to celebrate the big and small occasions of our lives. A home-baked cake says "welcome" to the everyday guest, and we mark the special days with cakes as well—from earliest childhood when we first blow out the candles on a birthday cake and make a silent, secret wish, to the big day when bride and groom join hands to cut the first symbolic slice of wedding cake. The appearance of a beautifully decorated cake and the accompanying rituals and ceremonies are the highlight of every birthday, anniversary, christening and wedding celebration. Often the look and taste of special cakes remain firmly embedded in our memories.

"I have never forgotten my early birthday cakes," writes James Beard. "Blessed with an insatiable taste for coconut, I always wanted a cake piled high with it. And since my birthday came in May, there were usually hawthorn blossoms available to decorate the plate. I felt that candles ruined the beauty of the cake and was firm about dispensing with the blowing out of candles ritual. These cakes under their white icing and coconut, were usually a sunshine or a moonshine cake or a white mountain cake." (*James Beard's American Cookery*.)

There are many traditional and symbolic cakes all over the world that are baked and served exclusively on certain holidays as part of a ritual celebration. Epiphany, on the twelfth night after Christmas, is celebrated all over France with the baking of the Twelfth-Night cake (*gâteau des rois*). Families and friends gather to celebrate the feast of the three kings—Melchior, Balthazar, and Gaspard—and the feasting ends with the arrival of a big cake in which is hidden a dried white bean. Whoever finds the bean is toasted and crowned king or queen for the day. This royal personage must then invite the assembled group to share a second *gâteau des rois* the following week. In this manner feasting may continue through the entire month of January. Similar customs are observed in other countries, with special cakes for New Year's Day.

Another traditional cake in France is the Christmas yule log, or *bûche de noël.* This is an elaborately decorated *génoise* cake that is rolled to resemble a yule log. There are special cakes to celebrate Easter, Name Days, Mother's Day, Election Day and many other occasions.

In Colonial America every housewife had her own treasured cache of cake recipes and women brought their own home-baked cakes to church socials, barn raisings, christenings, birthday parties, and weddings, as well as serving a slice of cake with mid-morning coffee, at afternoon teas and as special desserts.

All that baking was done, of course, at a time when there were no thermostatically controlled ovens or labor-saving devices such as the electric mixer. Many old recipes called for the cook (or, more likely, a young scullery maid) to beat butter and sugar together with a wooden spoon and then beat three or four eggs in, one at a time, beating for 15 minutes between each egg to make a light and frothy batter. A quick calculation shows that each cake would require a minimum of one hour's painful beating time. Today, an electric mixer, even a small portable one, accomplishes the same results in just a few minutes.

The two types of cake that rely for their leavening on the amount of air that is incorporated into the batter are the spongecake and the *génoise.* For those who like to bake their cakes as well as eat them, these two basic types of cake are well worth mastering. Spongecakes are light concoctions of sugar, eggs and flour and they contain no fat of any kind. The characteristic airy, even texture of the cake depends on the amount of air incorporated as the eggs and sugar are beaten, and on an even distribution of the flour. The spongecake batter can be baked in any one of a large number of shapes and sizes to make layer cakes, jelly rolls and ladyfingers.

The justly famous *génoise* is universally acclaimed as one of the finest products of the cakemaker's art. This French specialty is basically a spongecake that is enriched with sweet, fresh butter. It is a versatile cake indeed, and is the basis for a wide variety of layer cakes filled with rich butter creams and frosted according to the cakemaker's whim and taste. It may be baked in a flat rectangular shaped pan, cut into small diamonds and triangles and frosted to become the famous little cakes called *petits fours.* The same batter may also be baked in special molded pans to make a shell-shaped little cake called *madeleine.* This is the cake made famous round the world by Marcel Proust in his *Remembrance of Things Past:* "She sent for one of those short, plump little cakes called 'petites madeleines', which look as though they had been molded in the fluted scallop of the pilgrim's shell. And soon, mechanically, weary after a dull day with the prospect of a depressing morrow, I raised to my lips a spoonful of the cake . . . a shudder ran through my whole body and I stopped, intent upon the extraordinary changes that were taking place."

SPONGE-CAKES

A true spongecake contains no fat. It is made by whisking separated egg yolks and egg whites and sugar and folding in flour. Spongecake can also be made from whole eggs beaten over hot water. The characteristic airy, even texture of the cake depends on the amount of air incorporated during whisking and an even distribution of the flour. Therefore, the whisking must be correctly and thoroughly done; also a light hand is needed when folding in the flour so that the minimum amount of air is lost.

Spongecakes are meant for eating, not for keeping, and are best served the day they are baked. The absence of fat means that the cake becomes very dry after 2 or 3 days.

Preparation

Good organization is vital for perfect results when making spongecake. The ingredients must be at room temperature. Remove eggs from the refrigerator. For the whole-egg spongecake, let the eggs stand in their shells at room temperature for 1 hour. For a separated-egg spongecake, separate yolks and whites while the eggs are cold, then let them stand at room temperature for 1 hour.

Prepare the baking pans before starting to mix the batter. Preheat oven to the recommended temperature. Be sure that all equipment and mixing bowls are clean and free from grease.

The batter is delicate and must be baked as soon as it is prepared or valuable air, and therefore lightness, will be lost.

Equipment

You will need measuring cups and spoons to insure that the balance of ingredients is exact. Hit-or-miss measuring will produce poor results.

You will need a whisk. A balloon whisk is best as it gives the greatest volume. A rotary beater or electric mixer can be used if you prefer, and either will save time, but they will not give as much volume as the whisk.

A rubber spatula or scraper is needed for folding the flour into the mixture.

When preparing the baking pans for spongecake, always brush them with vegetable shortening. For layer-cake and flan pans, line them with a circle of wax paper, oil the paper, and then sprinkle with flour. Tap the pan lightly against a hard surface to distribute the flour evenly. Tap out any excess flour. This procedure prevents sticking, and will give the finished cake a crisp outer edge. When making a jelly roll, the pan must be lined, as shown in Lining a Jelly-Roll Pan (see Index).

When using the quick method all the whisking is done with the ingredients in a large bowl set over a saucepan of hot, not boiling, water. Make sure that the bowl you intend to use will sit on, and not in, the saucepan. Should the bowl touch the hot water, it would cause the eggs to set before they had been whisked. Use a large earthenware, china or glass bowl and a large saucepan, half-filled with water.

Ingredients

A spongecake is made with eggs, sugar, flour and flavorings. Compared with other cake mixtures, spongecakes contain a higher proportion of eggs and a smaller quantity of flour. The usual proportions are 1/4 cup flour and 2 tablespoons granulated sugar to each large egg used. The quantity of flour may be varied slightly, depending on how stiff a mix is required and the texture desired. For example, if the flour is slightly decreased, the results will be particularly light, provided the mixture is very carefully handled and baked. On the other hand, if the flour is slightly increased, the mixture will be firmer than usual and can be used to make small individual cakes.

Water is generally added to the mixture; a leavening agent or self-rising flour can also be used, depending on the type of cake required.

Eggs. The light texture of a spongecake is mainly due to the air trapped in the eggs during whisking; these thousands of tiny air bubbles act as the leavening. Large eggs are used to give the greatest volume. Ideally, they should be at least 3 days old and at room temperature. Always remove them from the refrigerator at least 1 hour before they are needed.

Sugar. Always use superfine granulated sugar when making a spongecake. These fine sugar crystals dissolve easily, which helps to give a smooth even texture. Avoid coarse sugars because they do not dissolve readily. Very fine sugars, such as confectioners' sugar, give the cake a hard crusty appearance. Make sure the sugar you use is dry and free from lumps. If in doubt, sieve it.

Flour. A classic spongecake uses all-purpose flour, as it gives a soft-textured cake. However, self-rising flour or the addition of a leavening agent to all-purpose flour is acceptable if an extra-light texture is required. Using self-rising flour means that the spongecake will have to be eaten on the day it is baked because a chemical leavening agent makes it quickly go stale.

Use flour at room temperature. Flour straight from the refrigerator will make a heavy spongecake. The cold flour will chill the egg and some of the trapped air will be released.

Additional Ingredients. Various extra ingredients can be incorporated into, or used to replace a quantity of, the basic mixture. Each additional ingredient must be added with care and always according to the recipe you are following to avoid upsetting the balance.

Cornstarch, arrowroot and rice flour can be used to replace a portion of the stated amount of flour. None of these starches contains gluten; therefore, any of them will have a softening effect, giving the cake crumb a more tender texture. When using any of these, use them to replace no more

Making a Separated-Egg Spongecake

8 to 10 portions

 6   eggs
1½   cups superfine granulated
        sugar
1½   cups sifted all-purpose flour
 1   teaspoon baking powder
 ½   teaspoon salt
 ⅓   cup cold water
 2   teaspoons vanilla extract
 2   teaspoons grated lemon
        rind

1 Separate eggs; there should be ½ cup yolks and ¾ cup whites.

2 Use an electric mixer to beat egg yolks until thick.

3 Beat in the sugar.

4 Beat in flour, baking powder and salt alternately with water, flavoring and grated rind.

5 Beat egg whites until stiff.

6 Fold egg-yolk mixture into the egg whites.

7 Pour into an ungreased tube pan, 10 × 4 inches. Bake at 325°F for 60 to 65 minutes.

8 Invert tube pan on a funnel and cool the cake.

than one third of the stated amount of flour.

Water. If 3 or more eggs are used, a little water may be added. This thins the mixture slightly and helps give a lighter sponge. As a rule, 1 tablespoon water is added to every 3 eggs used. The water should be warm.

Flavorings. Because the sponge mixture is delicate, heavy ingredients such as dried fruits and nuts are never used. The mixture is not stiff enough to hold them.

Grated lemon and orange rinds can both be used. Add grated rind to the eggs and stir the mixture lightly before starting to whisk it.

Other ingredients such as spices and powdered cocoa can be used to introduce different flavors.

If you are using a liquid flavoring, always consider the amount of liquid that you are introducing to the mixture. The liquid flavoring should be added in place of, never in addition to, the stated amount of water in a given recipe.

A flavoring should be concentrated because it is always added in small quantities.

• Rosewater or orange-flower water will give a delicate flavor.
• Extracts can be used, but remember that they should be added only in small amounts. Vanilla and almond extracts and liqueur flavors can all be used.
• Liqueurs such as kirsch or framboise and spirits such as rum or brandy give their characteristic flavors to a spongecake.
• Melted chocolate can be used where a dark chocolate flavor and color are required.

When using a powdered flavoring, sift it with the flour to make sure it is free from lumps and completely amalgamated with the flour.

Ground spices offer an easy way to flavor the basic mixture. Since they are used in very small quantities, it is not necessary to deduct the amount from the basic quantity of flour. Cinnamon, ginger, allspice and nutmeg are the 4 spices most frequently used.

Powdered cocoa can be added to give a chocolate flavor and color. Because this is used in amounts of over ½ ounce, a corresponding amount of flour must be deducted to preserve the balance of ingredients.

Methods of Making Spongecakes

There are several acceptable methods of preparing a spongecake. All have one thing in common: they incorporate as much air as possible during the whisking process.

The two main methods use the same principles, but in one method whole eggs are whisked and the other requires eggs to be separated. Whisking whole eggs over hot water is generally considered a quicker method.

Separated Egg Method. Separate eggs when cold, then let them warm to room temperature. Beat egg yolks until thick and lemon-colored. Gradually beat in sugar. Beat in flour, baking powder and salt alternately with water, flavorings and grated rind. Clean beaters and beat the egg whites until stiff. Fold the egg-yolk mixture into the egg whites. Pour the batter into an ungreased tube pan, 10 × 4 inches. Bake in a preheated 325°F oven for 60 to 65 minutes.

Whole Egg Method. Patience and time are needed to make a spongecake by this method, but it has some advantages. The cake can be stored for at least 2 days and it will be soft and light in texture.

Sift the flour, salt and any powdered flavorings together. Do this twice to aerate the ingredients as much as possible. Place the eggs in a large bowl and mix to blend them. Next add the total amount of sugar to the eggs and whisk together until the mixture is pale and creamy. Using a hand-held electric mixer will require about 15 minutes; by hand it will take at least 20 minutes. The aim is to dissolve the sugar in the eggs and to introduce as much air as possible. You will know when the mixture is ready because it will have doubled in volume and a whisk will leave a

trail when lifted out of the mixture and dribbled across the surface. The impression should remain for at least 3 seconds. The mixture is now ready for the flour to be incorporated.

Fold the sifted flour into the foamy mixture with a figure-eight action. Sprinkle about a quarter of the flour over the surface of the mixture; at the same time begin to fold in the flour, cutting through the mixture to incorporate the flour completely. Repeat with remaining flour until it has all been added. Never be tempted to stir the mixture or beat it as this would only result in a loss of the precious air, making a flat cake with a heavy texture. The mixture should have the same volume after the flour has been added as it did before adding it. A loss in volume at this stage cannot be corrected. Add any liquid flavoring or water at this stage by the same folding action. Without wasting time, quickly pour the mixture into the prepared pan and bake immediately as directed in the recipe.

Quick Method. The same procedure is followed with one major exception: the saucepan of hot water. By placing the eggs and sugar in a bowl over a saucepan of hot water, the heat from the water will help to dissolve the sugar more quickly and set the air as it is entrapped by the whisking. The quick method produces a soft, slightly sticky sponge with a light crust.

To prevent any delay, prepare the pan of hot water before you start whisking the eggs. Heat the water until it is boiling, then transfer the pan to a wooden board with a kitchen cloth on it to prevent slipping.

Add the bowl of eggs and continue as for the whole-egg method. It should take from 5 to 15 minutes for the mixture to reach a mousselike texture, 5 minutes with a hand-held electric mixer or 15 when the mixture is beaten by hand. As soon as the mixture is ready, remove the bowl from over the hot water. Whisk for another 5 minutes to cool the mixture. Fold in the flour in stages, as for the whole-egg method. The mixture will be of pouring consistency once all the flour, water (if used) and liquid flavoring are added.

Making a Whole-Egg Spongecake

makes two 8-inch layers

¾ cup sifted all-purpose flour
½ teaspoon baking powder
(optional)
flavoring
3 large eggs
6 tablespoons superfine sugar

1 Preheat oven (see chart). Prepare baking pan(s). Half-fill a large saucepan with water. Bring to a boil and remove from heat.

2 Sift flour, baking powder if using it, and dry flavoring twice. Place eggs in a large bowl and whisk together.

3 Add sugar to eggs and place bowl on top of saucepan of hot water. The bowl must not touch the water.

4 Whisk eggs and sugar together, using a whisk, rotary beater or electric mixer, until the mixer leaves a trail.

5 Remove bowl from saucepan and continue whisking until the mixture cools slightly and is pale in color.

6 Carefully but quickly fold in the flour, one quarter at a time, until it has all been incorporated.

7 Immediately pour batter into the prepared pan(s). Bake for required time. Do not open oven door during baking.

8 Press surface of cake lightly with fingertips. If cooked, it should feel firm and leave no impression.

Use a rubber spatula to scrape the mixture into the prepared pan.

Baking Spongecakes

A moderate oven is required for most spongecakes as this allows the air to expand fully before the egg sets (see chart).

Jelly rolls require a hotter oven than other cakes as quick baking is essential to keep the cake moist and pliable.

Always preheat the oven at least 15 minutes before you intend baking to insure the desired temperature. Bake at the recommended temperature or the results will be disappointing. If the oven is too hot, the air may rise too quickly, before the structure of the mix can support it, and the cake will sink in the center. On the other hand, the egg may set before the air has a chance to expand fully, and this will result in a close, heavy texture.

Never allow the mixture to sit in the pan waiting for the oven, as the volume that you have worked hard to produce will begin to break down. Place the cake in the heated oven, usually in the center, and close the door carefully. Slamming the oven door will cause a sudden jar to the mixture and break down some of the bubbles. Do not be tempted to open the oven door until the recommended baking time is over, as this could also cause the cake to sink in the center.

When the recommended baking time is over, test the cake for doneness by pressing the surface lightly with the fingertips. If the cake is baked, it should feel firm and the fingertips should leave no impression. The cake should have shrunk from the sides of the pan and there should be no sound of bubbling.

Cooling. As soon as the cake is baked, remove the cake pan from the oven and stand it on a damp cloth towel for no longer than 30 seconds. This helps to loosen the cake from the pan. When making a jelly roll, this rule does not apply.

If cake is level with top of pan, invert on a wire rack and carefully peel away the lining paper. Turn the cake

Pan Sizes, Baking Times and Temperatures

For Whole-Egg Sponge Cakes

Number of eggs	Size of cake pan	Oven temperature	Baking time in minutes
2	two 7-inch round	350°F	20 to 25
	one 8-inch round	350°F	25 to 30
	one jelly roll, 11 × 7 inches	400°F	8 to 10
	one 8-inch flan	350°F	25 to 30
3	three 7-inch layers	350°F	20 to 25
	two 8-inch layers	350°F	25 to 30
	one jelly roll, 13 × 9 inches	400°F	8 to 10
	one 6-inch springform	350°F 325°F	25, then 40

over so that it is now right side up again and leave it until completely cool. If cake has risen above the top of pan, invert the pan over a slender-necked bottle and let hang until cool.

Layer Cakes

The traditional spongecake makes a delicious layer cake when split and filled with cream and/or jam, or another soft filling. You can bake the cake in 2 or more shallow layer-cake pans, or use 1 deep cake pan and split the cold baked cake horizontally into 2 layers. Or you can split a deep cake into 3 or 4 rounds. Alternatively you can bake the cake in a shallow rectangular pan. In this case, the baked cake is cut across into equal pieces that are assembled, one on top of the other, with a filling between the layers.

A spongecake simply filled with jam or cream looks perfect just dusted with confectioners' sugar.

For a rich taste, the cake may be lightly soaked in sugar syrup, plain or laced with brandy or rum, the whole cake smothered with whipped cream, then decorated with toasted sliced almonds. The sides and top of the cake may be decorated in many other ways.

Jelly Rolls

Jelly rolls and flan cases are made with a spongecake mixture because it is so light and soft in texture. It is a mixture that will roll easily after baking, essential for jelly rolls. Making a sponge roll is simple once you know how, but there are a few rules that insure success. While the spongecake is baking, place a large sheet of wax paper, at least 1 inch larger all around than the baking pan, on a cloth towel. Sprinkle the paper heavily with superfine sugar. If you are using jam as a filling, warm the jam in a small saucepan.

Rolling and Filling Jelly Rolls. As soon as the cake is baked, invert it on the sheet of sugared wax paper. Peel away the lining paper. Using a long-bladed sharp knife, cut away a ¼-inch strip of cake from all sides. These edges are crisp and if left on they will hamper the rolling.

Make a cut halfway through the cake 1 inch in, and parallel to, that end from which the cake is to be rolled. This gets the rolling off to an even start. Working quickly, spread the jam or other filling over the cake up to 1 inch from the edges.

To make a firm start, press the

Lining a Jelly-Roll Pan

1 Place pan on a large sheet of wax paper and draw around the base of the pan.

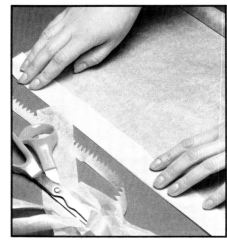

2 Cut the paper 1 inch out from the line you have drawn. Crease paper on the line.

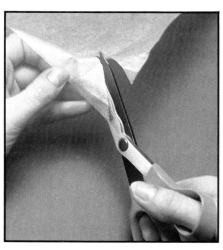

3 Oil the pan and press the paper down into the pan. Cut and mold the corners.

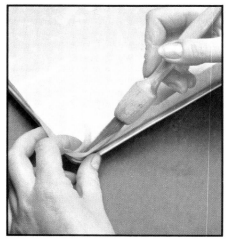

4 Brush the surface of the wax paper with oil.

half-cut end up and over and hold it down with one hand; with the other hand grip the wax paper. Working away from you, roll the spongecake firmly to make an even roll. With the paper still around the roll, hold the cake firmly to set for a second or two. Remove the wax paper and place the roll, seam side down, on a wire cooling rack.

For a jelly roll filled with cream or butter cream, omit the jam and roll the cake, with the wax paper inside. Allow the cake to cool completely. Carefully unroll the cake; discard the wax paper. Spread the cake with the required filling. These creamy fillings would melt if spread on the roll when it is hot.

Mini Rolls. To make mini jelly rolls, bake the cake as usual, turn out, and trim. Then cut the cake lengthwise into halves to make 2 long rectangles. Spread each with jam and roll up, starting at the longer sides to make 2 long narrow rolls. When the rolls are com-

pletely cold, cut each into even-size lengths.

Decorating Jelly Rolls. The quickest way to decorate a jelly roll is to dust it with superfine sugar or sift confectioners' sugar over it. Alternatively, the cake can be covered with any of a variety of icings to turn it into something special.

• Cover the roll completely with melted chocolate; sprinkle along the top with nuts or chocolate sprinkles while the chocolate is still soft. Allow chocolate to set completely before serving.
• Cover the roll with white icing, colored and/or flavored.
• Drizzle the top of the roll with white icing and let it dribble down the sides. When the icing is on the point of setting, decorate with a row of sliced candied fruit and/or chopped nuts.
• Spoon or pipe whipped cream in a decorative design over the roll and decorate with fresh strawberries, raspberries or blueberries.

Flan Bases

Like jelly roll, spongecake flan bases are usually made with a whisked sponge mixture. The batter is baked in a depressed fluted pan so that when the cake is baked and inverted, the flutes and depression in the pan form the shape of the flan, which will hold a filling and act as a case.

Filling Spongecake Flans. Fillings for flan bases are numerous, but they are always precooked and cooled fillings, or not cooked at all. Any filling should be added as close to serving time as possible to keep the sponge from becoming soggy if the filling is moist. Another important point to be considered is appearance. Whatever the filling, it should be neat, decorative and appealing.

Fresh fruit makes a mouthwatering treat when arranged well. To prevent sogginess in the cake base, brush the inside with warmed jam before filling it with fruit. Choose fruit that is juicy on the inside yet fairly dry on the outside to guard against ruining the

Making a Jelly Roll

1 While the spongecake is baking, cut a piece of wax paper slightly larger than the jelly-roll pan.

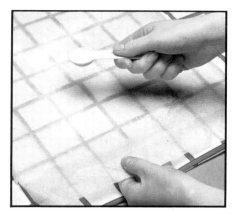

2 Place the wax paper on a cloth towel. Sprinkle paper with 2 tablespoons superfine sugar.

3 If using jam for a filling, warm 4 tablespoons jam in a small saucepan.

4 Invert baked spongecake on the sugared wax paper. Peel away lining paper.

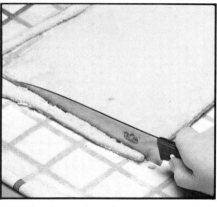

5 Cut ¼ inch from all edges. This removes crisp portions and makes rolling easier.

6 Make a cut halfway through the cake, 1 inch from, and parallel to, the end to be rolled.

7 Working quickly, spread the jam over the cake to 1 inch from the edges.

8 To make a firm start, press cut end over and hold down with one hand. Grip paper with other hand.

9 Working away from you, make an even roll. Hold the paper around the roll for a few seconds.

texture. Once the base has been filled, coat the fruit with a little melted and sieved jam or jelly to serve as a glaze. This makes the surface shiny and keeps the fruit from drying or appearing dry.

Canned fruit can be used in place of fresh fruit if it has been well drained and dried on paper towels.

To add variety, fruit may be arranged over a layer of whipped cream, butter cream or sweetened whipped cream cheese. Another possibility is to mix the sweetened whipped cream cheese with the fruit before filling the flan.

After a fruit filling has been glazed, sprinkle it with toasted nuts.

Storing and Freezing Spongecakes

Spongecakes, whatever their form, made by these methods are at their best when eaten on the day they are made. If necessary, an unfilled and undecorated cake may be stored in an airtight tin for up to 2 days.

Never attempt to freeze an unbaked spongecake mixture as it will not be edible. When baked but unfilled, a whisked spongecake can be stored in the freezer for up to 6 months, if wrapped tightly in heavy-duty freezer wrap. To serve a frozen spongecake, thaw it in the freezer wrappings at room temperature for 1 to 2 hours. Unwrap and fill as desired.

GÉNOISES

Génoise cakes are made for special occasions. Deliciously light and buttery, they are rightly considered the queen of spongecakes. Génoise is a moist versatile cake. It can be used for *petits fours*, madeleines, cheesecakes

and many other delicious desserts. Its special qualities of richness and lightness are made by adding melted clarified butter to a whisked spongecake mixture. Génoise needs a slightly longer baking time than fat-free spongecakes, and it will keep better because of the fat.

There are 2 basic génoise recipes: *génoise fine* and *génoise commune*. As the name suggests, the *fine* is richer than the *commune*. They are both made with the same quantities of eggs and sugar, but *génoise commune* uses half the quantity of butter and more flour to compensate.

A third member of the génoise family is called *biscuit fin au beurre*. This is made by a slightly different method. Whereas in the other two cake batters whole eggs and sugar are whisked together over hot water, in *biscuit fin au beurre* the yolks of the eggs are whisked with the sugar in a warm bowl and then the egg whites are folded in with the flour before the butter is added. This cuts down the overall beating time by about half. When baked, the cake has a less fluffy texture than *génoise fine* or *commune*. It is used mostly for cakes that are to be iced, because it gives a firmer surface on which to work.

Ingredients for Génoise

Génoise contains eggs, sugar, flour and butter.

Eggs. These should always be medium-size and used whole. The light texture that is associated with a génoise is achieved by the rising properties of the whisked eggs. The eggs also give a golden color to the cake.

Always use eggs at room temperature. Remove them from the refrigerator at least 1 hour before they are needed. If time is short and does not permit an hour's wait, then break the eggs into a bowl and set the bowl in a container of lukewarm water for 15 minutes.

Sugar. Only superfine sugar is suitable; granulated sugar will not dissolve quickly enough and would result in a coarse, heavy texture.

Flour. A fine cake flour is the perfect choice. Self-rising flour is unsuitable as all the necessary rise comes from the whisked eggs. In the absence of fine cake flour, add a little cornstarch to all-purpose flour to produce a finer-textured sponge. Use approximately 1 tablespoon cornstarch for each ¾ cup all-purpose flour.

Butter. Butter is the only suitable fat for a génoise. Do not be tempted to use margarine; it has neither the fine flavor of butter nor the correct amount of water. Margarine contains too much water, which evaporates on melting, causing an immediate loss of volume and a heavy texture to the cake.

Always use unsalted butter. Butter must be clarified. Melt it carefully so that it does not overheat or separate. Skim foam from the top. Cool slightly, then spoon off the oily liquid, leaving the milky whey in the pan. Use only the oily liquid, the butterfat, in a cake batter. (See Volume 7 Index for Clarified Butter.)

Flavorings. A basic génoise has a delicate buttery flavor that does not *need* any additional flavoring. There is no reason, however, why you should not experiment.

The traditional flavoring for a génoise is orange-flower water. It is used in very small quantities, usually 1 teaspoon for each 4 eggs, to impart only a slight hint of flavor. An alternative is finely grated orange or lemon rind, again in very small quantities, no more than 1 teaspoon for each 4 eggs. Any more will result in a sticky cake.

An unusual though traditional method of flavoring is to place 2 small sweet rose or lemon verbena leaves on the base of the prepared cake pan before pouring in the cake mixture. This adds just the correct amount of subtle flavoring to a plain génoise cake.

Chocolate. Melted chocolate can be added to give a rich chocolate flavor; use up to 3 ounces (3 squares) for a 4-egg génoise. Add it alternately with the butter and take special care to do this slowly to avoid formation of any lumps of chocolate.

Alternatively, use powdered cocoa, substituting 2 tablespoons cocoa for the same amount of sifted flour. Sift it with the flour before folding it in. These proportions work for small amounts of ingredients.

Nuts. Ground nuts, up to 2 ounces (½ cup) for a 4-egg génoise, can be added for a rich texture. Ground almonds and hazelnuts are the most popular nuts for a génoise because they complement the buttery flavor of the spongecake.

Spices. Use only in very small quantities to complement the buttery flavor rather than overwhelming it. Never use more than ½ teaspoon of any of the following: ground allspice, cinnamon, cloves, ginger or nutmeg.

Pans for Génoise

The only special equipment needed for génoise is the pan. The traditional pan is called in French a *moule à manqué,* which can be loosely translated as a "foolproof mold." This pan is round with sides slightly sloping outward toward the rim; it is approximately 2 inches deep. The cake when turned out has slightly sloping sides, down which the icing runs quickly and easily. This gives an attractive shape, particularly effective when iced.

Deep cake pans are rarely used because a génoise is a very light cake that could not support itself in a deep pan. Layer-cake pans or flan pans, now being imported from France with a diameter of 10 inches or more, can be used as well as fancy molds, individual cake pans and tart pans.

Small cakes called madeleines are a classic of the génoise type. These are baked in shallow, shell-shaped molds, which form a set in a single pan. They are available in a variety of sizes. When baked, the cakes resemble shells; they are served upside down to show off the shape. (A heavier batter, however, more like a poundcake batter, is sometimes used for madeleines.)

Brush the inside of the pans lightly with melted butter and put aside until the butter is just on the point of setting and a cloudy film is visible. Using a sieve, sift in a little flour. Shake the pan to make sure that a fine film of flour covers the pan and shake out any excess flour. Take care not to overflour the pan or a hard crust will form on the outside of the cake, which will cause the delicate sponge to crack when cut.

Making a Génoise

Génoise mixtures must be prepared and baked immediately if they are to be light and buttery. Get thoroughly organized before you start. The first job is to remove eggs from the refrigerator to allow them to come to room temperature. Preheat the oven, allowing 10 to 15 minutes for it to reach the desired temperature. Check that the oven shelf is positioned in the center, unless you are using a convection oven, in which case the position of the shelf will not matter.

Next check that you have all the necessary equipment on hand. Prepare the cake pans. Check that you have all the ingredients ready before you start.

Careful attention is the secret of a successful génoise. You need a light hand in the whisking and folding. The method for both kinds of génoise is the same.

Melting the butter. Dice the butter and put it in a small bowl over hot, not boiling, water until it has just melted. Do not let it overheat. Turn off the heat; the warmth of the bowl will keep the butter from resolidifying. Clarify the butter. Measure the oily liquid after it has been clarified.

Sifting the flour. Sift the flour and cornstarch together. This insures even distribution of the cornstarch and introduces extra air, which helps the cake to rise.

Whisking. Place the eggs, usually 4 medium-size eggs to every 9 tablespoons of superfine sugar, in a mixing bowl. Set the bowl over a saucepan of hot, not boiling, water. A low heat under the saucepan provides just the right temperature. Whisk the eggs and sugar together so they are well blended. If using a hand-held electric mixer, this first mixing can be done on low speed. Once the mixture is blended, continue whisking at a higher speed. The mixture gradually turns from a golden egg color to pale yellow. Continue whisking until the mixture has doubled in bulk, resembles whipped cream, and will just hold its shape when the whisk is lifted above the bowl.

If any of the mixture gathers around the side of the bowl, scrape this down with a spatula or it will set with the heat from the water and be unusable.

Cooling. As soon as the mixture has reached this stage, it should be removed from the top of the saucepan and placed on a steady surface to cool. A wooden board is ideal.

By now whisking will have introduced thousands of tiny air bubbles into the eggs and sugar. To save these bubbles and to help the mixture cool quickly, continue to whisk until the side of the bowl is no longer warm to the touch. This will take approximately 3 minutes.

Folding. The next step is to fold the cornstarch-flour mixture evenly into the eggs. Sprinkle a little of the sifted mixture over the surface of the eggs. Then, using a figure-eight motion, cut the flour mixture down into the bowl so the flour slips gently off the side of the spoon.

Continue adding the flour mixture, a little at a time, until all the flour has been added and there is no visible floury look on the surface of the batter. Never be tempted to hurry this process by beating or stirring in the flour because either of these will break down the precious air bubbles, thereby reducing the overall volume of the cake.

Adding the Butter. Add only a spoonful of the liquefied butter at a time and again use the folding figure-eight motion. Take the spoon right to the base of the bowl before turning it, so that all the butter moves through the mixture. Never add more than a spoonful at a time—or you may have difficulty making the butter blend in—and add more only when you are sure the previous spoonful has been completely incorporated.

If the mixture is overworked at this crucial stage, it will liquefy and turn a greenish color. The only thing to be done then is to throw it away and start again.

As soon as the flour and butter are safely folded in, immediately pour the mixture into the cake pan. If a trace of butter appears on top of the mixture in the pan, it may be pressed in with a single stroke of the spoon. Bake at once.

Biscuit Fin au Beurre

The method for making *biscuit fin au beurre* is slightly different from that for the other 2 génoise spongecakes, and considerably quicker. The eggs are separated at the outset and the yolks are whisked with the sugar in a warm bowl, but not over heat, until thick and pale.

The volume and lightness come from the egg whites, which are whisked separately until they form soft peaks. These are then folded into the yolk mixture; sift in the flour mixture at the same time, with the same important folding action used before. The butter is folded in at the end, in the same manner. The batter must be baked at once.

Baking Times for Génoise

These vary according to the type of pan that is used, but a génoise usually needs 25 to 30 minutes to bake. Always bake the cake in the center of the oven unless the recipe states otherwise.

Never be tempted to open the oven door once the cake is inside, as a sudden rush of cold air into the hot oven can make the cake sink in the center.

The génoise will be cooked to perfection when it is evenly risen, is soft but firm to the touch, and has a rich golden brown color. If you are unsure whether the cake is ready, insert a very fine skewer or cake tester into the center. When lifted out, it should be clean, with no uncooked cake batter adhering to it. If the cake is not done, return it to

Making a Génoise

The ingredients listed here are for *génoise fine,* which is the richer and more aristocratic of the two types of génoise.

Génoise commune is made with less butter and so has a firmer surface. It is used mostly for cakes that are to be iced. The methods for both kinds of génoise are the same.

To make a *génoise commune,* use the same quantities of eggs, cornstarch and sugar listed here, but use 1 cup all-purpose flour and only 4 tablespoons butter.

one 8-inch cake, 6 portions

7 tablespoons unsalted butter
¾ cup sifted all-purpose flour
1 tablespoon cornstarch
4 medium-size eggs
9 tablespoons superfine sugar

 Whisk eggs and sugar together until blended. Use low speed if using an electric mixer.

 Increase speed until mixture doubles in bulk and turns pale. Remove from heat. Whisk until cool.

the oven and bake for 3 minutes more at a time until it is baked.

Génoise for Small Cakes

A génoise provides the perfect base for a selection of small cakes. Any of the basic recipes for génoise can be used. Make the cake and bake it in a jelly-roll pan. Cut the large cake into individual cakes. Because a génoise is a little special, the decorations for small cakes made of this batter also need to be special to be worthy of the cake.

• Cut the génoise into 2-inch rounds. Split each round horizontally. Sandwich the layers together with a circle of almond paste cut to fit the layer exactly. Cover the cake entirely with coffee-flavored butter icing (see Volume 1 Index). Sprinkle toasted chopped almonds over the top and sides of the cake. Sift confectioners' sugar and powdered cocoa over each cake, then finish off with a large piped swirl of whipped cream or butter icing in the center of the cake. Repeat with remaining cake rounds.

1 Preheat oven to 375°F. Prepare an 8-inch layer-cake pan by buttering, then flouring.

2 Dice the butter and melt in a small bowl over a pan of hot water. Remove from heat, cool, and clarify.

3 Sift flour and cornstarch together. Place eggs and sugar in a bowl over a saucepan of hot, not boiling, water.

6 Sprinkle on a little of the flour mixture. Fold in flour mixture in spoonfuls with a figure-eight motion.

7 Fold in butter, 1 spoonful at a time, with the same motion, until it is all incorporated.

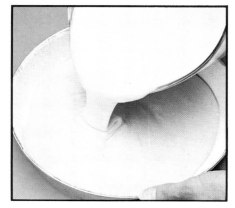

8 Immediately pour the mixture into the pan. Bake in the center of the oven for 25 to 30 minutes.

• Cut génoise into 2-inch rounds, then cut each round into 3 layers. Sandwich the cakes together with Chocolate Butter Cream (see Index) to which crushed crisp macaroons have been added. Spread a thin layer of the butter cream to cover the cakes completely. Lay plain chocolate curls in one direction over the top of each cake. Place your finger just above the cake and sift confectioners' sugar on top. Remove your finger and a strip of the chocolate curls will remain plain.

• Cut génoise into 1½-inch squares and prick each square with a fork. Drizzle with a little cream sherry and allow it to soak into the cake. Cover each cake entirely with delicately piped swirls of whipped cream, then sprinkle the cake with a few chopped pistachios.

• Cut a large génoise into diamond-shaped pieces and cut each diamond into 2 layers. Sandwich each cake together with Vanilla Butter Cream (see Index). Spread the sides of the cakes with butter cream and dip into grated chocolate. Place 2 cubes of candied pineapple and a candied cherry on top of each cake and cover with White Icing (see Index).

• Homemade ladyfingers are excellent for lining charlotte molds, making the base for a trifle, or for serving with ice creams and sorbets. To make ladyfingers, prepare the basic quantity of *biscuit fin au beurre* and preheat the oven. Use a pastry bag fitted with a plain piping tip, and pipe the batter onto a buttered and floured baking sheet as you would for éclairs. Bake for 20 to 25 minutes, until firm and rather dry.

Black Forest Cake

10 to 12 portions

8 medium-size eggs
1¼ cups superfine granulated
    sugar
¼ cup powdered cocoa
1½ cups sifted all-purpose flour
⅞ cup melted clarified butter

Filling and Decoration

2 cans (16 ounces each)
    pitted dark sweet cherries
2 teaspoons arrowroot

6 tablespoons kirsch
3 cups heavy cream
4 ounces semisweet chocolate

1 Preheat oven to 350°F. Make 2 génoise layers, substituting cocoa for cornstarch.

2 Bake cakes for 25 to 30 minutes, until well risen. Cool in pans for 3 minutes, then invert on wire racks.

3 Drain syrup from cherries. Reserve 12 perfect cherries and ½ cup syrup. Halve the remaining cherries.

4 Blend arrowroot with 2 tablespoons of reserved syrup. Boil with rest of syrup; stir till clear. Add halved cherries; cool.

5 Cut each cake into 2 layers. Put bottom layer on serving dish. Drizzle 1 tablespoon kirsch over each of 4 layers.

6 Whip cream to soft peaks. Stir in 2 tablespoons kirsch. Put some cream in a pastry bag with a big star tip.

7 Spread bottom layer and next 2 layers with half of cream. Add a third of halved cherries and syrup to each layer.

8 Place undecorated layer on top. Spread remaining cream over top and sides of cake to cover completely.

9 Shave chocolate with vegetable peeler to make curls. Pipe rosettes with reserved cream. Decorate cake with whole cherries and chocolate curls.

Chocolate Scroll Cake

6 to 8 portions

6 ounces (6 squares) semisweet chocolate, melted
4 medium-size eggs
9 tablespoons superfine granulated sugar
¾ cup sifted all-purpose flour

1 tablespoon cornstarch
7 tablespoons melted clarified butter
Chocolate Butter Cream (recipe follows)
¼ to ½ cup confectioners' sugar

Preheat oven to 375°F. Prepare an 8-inch layer-cake pan. Melt 3 ounces of the chocolate and let it cool. Make the cake, following the directions for Génoise (see Index), adding the melted chocolate alternately with the melted butter. Cool the cake in the pan for 3 minutes, then invert it on a wire cooling rack.

While the cake is cooling, make the chocolate butter cream. Chill it. Use remaining chocolate to make chocolate scrolls. Carefully transfer the scrolls to a wire rack and place in the refrigerator to become firm while assembling the cake.

Cut the cold cake into 3 horizontal layers and sandwich them together with about one quarter of the cooled butter cream. Place the cake on a serving plate. Cover the top and sides of the cake with remaining butter cream and smooth the surface. Lay the larger perfect chocolate scrolls in one direction on top of the cake. Use the smaller scrolls and broken pieces to cover the sides of the cake, arranging them haphazardly.

Cut four 1-inch strips of wax paper as long as the diameter of the cake. Lay them at intervals across the cake, at right angles to the lines of scrolls. Sift confectioner's sugar over the cake, then remove the strips of wax paper.

Variation: For a Normandy cake, make a *génoise fine.* When cold, split into 2 layers and drizzle 2 tablespoons Calvados (apple brandy) or applejack over the bottom layer. Spread 5 tablespoons sweetened applesauce on the brandy-soaked layer. Top with 1 cup Pastry Cream (see Volume 4 Index) and place the top layer over the cream. Brush with apricot glaze. Make a glaze with 1½ cups confectioners' sugar and 1 tablespoon Calvados. Color lightly with green food coloring. Pour glaze over the cake and down the sides. Decorate with sliced almonds, arranged in a fan pointing into the cake. Set a half green grape or candied green cherry in the center of the fan.

Chocolate Butter Cream

about 1 cup

6 ounces unsalted butter
½ cup confectioners' sugar
2 medium-size egg yolks

2 ounces (2 squares) semisweet chocolate

Soften 3 ounces of the butter. Cut the rest into pieces and keep it cold. Combine sugar and egg yolks in a bowl and beat with a whisk, rotary beater or electric mixer until the eggs form a ribbon when the beater is lifted. Add the softened butter, while continuing to beat. Meanwhile melt the choco-late over hot water, and cool it. Beat the cooled chocolate into the butter cream, then add the cold butter, piece by piece, until the mixture is smooth. Chill butter cream until it reaches the right texture for spreading. Then use at once, or refrigerate for up to three days.

White Praline for Icing

about ⅓ cup

3 ounces lump sugar
5 tablespoons water

6 tablespoons ground almonds

Dissolve the sugar in the water in a small pan. Boil to the hard-ball stage, 248°F on a candy thermometer. Remove from heat and stir in the ground almonds. Stir until the mixture is sandy and crumbly. The praline mixture may be made in a double quantity and the unused portion can be stored in an airtight tin.

To decorate cakes, shake the praline through a sieve over the top of a cake.

Chocolate Spongecake

6 portions

5 tablespoons butter, softened	3 eggs, separated
10 tablespoons sifted all-purpose flour	7 tablespoons superfine granulated sugar
3½ ounces (3½ squares) semisweet chocolate	⅛ teaspoon salt confectioners' sugar (optional)
2 tablespoons prepared coffee, or water	½ cup vanilla or chocolate butter icing (optional)

Preheat oven to 350°F. Use 1 tablespoon of the butter to coat a shallow 8-inch-square cake pan. Sprinkle in 1 tablespoon of the flour and tip and rotate the pan to distribute flour evenly. Shake out any excess flour and set the pan aside.

Break the chocolate into pieces and place in a small saucepan with the coffee or water. Set over very low heat and melt the chocolate, stirring occasionally. As soon as chocolate is melted, remove pan from heat. With a wooden spoon gradually beat remaining butter into the chocolate. Cool the mixture to lukewarm. Meanwhile, in a mixing bowl beat the egg yolks lightly with a wire whisk, rotary beater or electric mixer. Gradually beat in all but 1 tablespoon of the sugar. Continue beating until the mixture is pale yellow and will make a ribbon trail on itself when the whisk is lifted. With a wire whisk, rotary beater or electric mixer, beat the egg whites and salt together in another bowl. When soft peaks are formed, add remaining sugar to egg whites and beat until stiff.

Blend the chocolate mixture into the egg-yolk batter. With a rubber scraper, carefully fold in one quarter of the egg whites. When partly blended, sift in one quarter of remaining flour and continue blending. Add another quarter of egg whites followed by another quarter of the flour. Repeat until all egg whites and flour have been added and well blended.

Pour the batter into the prepared pan. Bake in the middle of the oven for 30 minutes, until a skewer inserted in the center of the cake comes out dry and clean. The cake will rise about ¼ inch above the rim of the pan and the top will split. Remove pan from the oven and cool the cake in the pan for 5 minutes. The cake will sink slightly. To remove cake from the pan, run a knife around the inside of the pan. Place a wire rack on top of the pan, turn both over together, and shake so the cake slides out of the pan onto the rack. Cool the cake for about 2½ hours.

Serve the cake sprinkled with confectioners' sugar or filled and topped with butter icing (see Volume 1 Index).

Blotkake

(Norwegian Spongecake with Raspberries)

8 portions

Norwegian Spongecake

1 teaspoon butter
6 large eggs
1 cup superfine granulated
   sugar
1 teaspoon vanilla extract
1¼ cups sifted self-rising flour

Filling and Topping

2 cups heavy cream
¼ cup superfine granulated
   sugar
1 pint fresh raspberries

Preheat oven to 350°F. Lightly grease a loose-bottomed 9-inch round cake pan or springform pan with the butter. Line the bottom of the pan with parchment or wax paper.

Break 4 whole eggs into a large mixing bowl. Separate yolks and whites of remaining 2 eggs. Add yolks to the whole eggs and reserve the whites in a separate bowl. Add the sugar and vanilla to the eggs; with a wire whisk, rotary beater or electric mixer, beat until the mixture is thick and pale yellow. Lightly sift the flour into the egg and sugar batter and blend it in with a rubber scraper. Beat the egg whites with a wire whisk or rotary beater until they form stiff peaks. Gradually add the whites to the batter and fold them in. Turn the mixture into the cake pan and place in the center of the oven. After 10 minutes, reduce oven heat to 325°F and bake the cake for 50 minutes longer, until it is done. Test by inserting a skewer into the center; if it comes out clean, the cake is ready. Remove the cake from the oven and let it stand for 5 minutes

before removing it from the pan. Place cake on a wire rack and let it cool.

Pour the cream and half of the sugar into a mixing bowl. With a wire whisk or rotary beater, whip the cream until it thickens and forms soft peaks. Quickly wash raspberries, drain, and place on paper towels to dry.

When the cake is completely cooled, carefully cut it with a long sharp knife into 3 layers of equal depth. Place one cake layer on a serving dish. With a table knife, spread a ½-inch layer of whipped cream over the cake. Place the second layer on top of the cream, and spread with another ½-inch layer of cream. Set the third layer in place and leave the top plain. Spread some of remaining cream on the sides of the cake. Place remainder in a pastry bag fitted with a star tip and pipe an attractive border around the top rim and the base. Completely cover the top with the raspberries mixed with remaining sugar.

Génoise with Hazelnuts

8 to 10 portions

3 tablespoons unsalted butter
⅔ cup sifted all-purpose flour
4 ounces hazelnuts, toasted
    (1 cup)
4 medium-size eggs
9 tablespoons superfine
    granulated sugar

pinch of salt
1 cup Vanilla Butter Cream
    (see Index)
Confectioners' Sugar Glaze
    (see Index)

Preheat oven to 375°F. Prepare a 9-inch layer-cake pan by buttering and sifting flour over it. Melt the butter in a small bowl set over a pan of hot water; set aside. Sift the flour. Grind 3 ounces (¾ cup) of the hazelnuts.

Separate the eggs and put the yolks and sugar in a warm bowl. Whisk until thick. Fold in half of the ground nuts. Whisk the egg whites with the pinch of salt until they form soft peaks. Fold the egg whites and flour alternately by spoonful into the egg yolks. Quickly fold in the melted butter and turn the batter into the prepared pan. Bake for 25 to 30 minutes, until done. Leave the cake in the pan for 3 minutes, then invert on a wire rack to cool.

Make the butter cream and stir in the remaining ground hazelnuts. Split the cold cake into 2 layers. Sandwich the layers together with one third of the butter cream. Spoon another third into a pastry bag fitted with a star tip. Make the glaze and flavor it with vanilla extract. At once pour the glaze into the middle of the cake and spread to cover just the top. Leave it to set.

Use remaining butter cream to coat the sides of the cake. Chop remaining hazelnuts for decoration and press them into the sides of the cake. Pipe a shell border of butter cream around the top of the cake.

Almond Mocha Cake

8 to 10 portions

4 medium-size eggs
9 tablespoons superfine
    granulated sugar
¾ cup sifted all-purpose flour
1 tablespoon cornstarch
7 tablespoons unsalted butter

2 cups Vanilla Butter Cream
    (see Index)
2 tablespoons prepared strong coffee
3 ounces blanched almonds,
    slivered (¾ cup)
¼ cup confectioners' sugar,
    approximately

Preheat oven to 375°F. Prepare an 8-inch layer-cake pan. Make and bake the cake, following the directions for Génoise (see Index). Cool the cake in the pan for 3 minutes, then invert it on a wire rack.

Make the butter cream, beating in the coffee after half of the butter has been added. Chill the butter cream until ready to use it. Spread the almonds in a skillet and stir over low heat until golden brown. Cool the almonds.

With a long-bladed sharp knife cut the cake into 2 horizontal layers. Place the bottom layer on a serving plate. Spread a quarter of the butter cream over the bottom layer, then place the second layer on top. Put 4 tablespoons of the butter cream in a pastry bag fitted with a medium-size star tip and set aside. Use remaining butter cream to cover the top and sides of the cake. Sprinkle the shredded almonds over the top and sides. Sift enough confectioners' sugar over to cover the cake lightly. Pipe 8 swirls of butter cream around the outer top edge of the cake.

Variations: For *gâteau Cendrillon* (coffee Cinderella cake), add 1 tablespoon prepared strong coffee to the eggs, then make a *génoise fine*. Make Vanilla Butter Cream (see Index) and flavor it with 1 tablespoon Tia Maria or Kahlúa. Reserve one third of the butter cream in a pastry bag fitted with a star tip. Slice the cold cake into 2 layers. Sandwich layers together with remaining butter cream. Brush the cake with apricot glaze. Make Confectioners' Sugar Glaze (see Index), dissolving ½ teaspoon instant coffee powder in the water. Glaze the cake, then decorate with swirls of butter cream and top each swirl with a browned hazelnut.

For Viennese orange cake, make a *génoise fine*. When cold, slice the cake into 2 layers. Make Pastry Cream (see Volume 4 Index) and flavor with grated orange rind. Sandwich the layers with pastry cream and pour Confectioners' Sugar Glaze (see Index) over the top. Decorate with blanched strips of orange rind.

Povoa Almond Cake

8 to 10 portions

1 teaspoon vegetable oil
6 eggs, separated
½ cup superfine granulated
   sugar
6 ounces ground almonds
   (1 cup)

2 tablespoons milk
   White Icing (see Index)
¼ teaspoon almond extract
2 ounces slivered almonds
   (½ cup)

Preheat oven to 350°F. Line a jelly-roll pan 10 × 15 inches with nonstick silicone or wax paper. Brush the paper with the teaspoon of oil.

Place the egg yolks and sugar in a mixing bowl. Beat the mixture with a wire whisk, rotary beater or electric mixer until thick and pale. Use a large metal spoon to fold in the ground almonds and the milk. Set the batter aside. Beat the egg whites in another bowl with a whisk, beater or mixer until they form stiff peaks. With the metal spoon gently but thoroughly fold the egg whites into the batter. Pour the mixture into the prepared pan, smoothing it over with the back of the spoon.

Place the pan in the oven and bake for 15 to 20 minutes, until the cake is lightly browned and comes away from the sides of the pan. Remove pan from oven and let the cake cool for 5 minutes. Carefully turn the cake out on a flat surface covered with wax paper, sprinkled with a little cornstarch. Remove and discard the paper lining from the cake and set the cake aside to cool completely.

Make the white icing, and stir in the almond extract. Let the icing cool to room temperature.

When the cake is cold, cut it crosswise into 4 rectangles, using a sharp knife. Place 1 rectangle on a serving platter. Using a spatula, spread one sixth of the icing on the cake and top with another rectangle. Make alternate layers with remaining cake and icing. Spread remaining icing evenly over the top and sides of the cake. Sprinkle the slivered almonds over the icing and serve the cake at once.

White Icing

about 2 cups

1 pound confectioners' sugar
   (4 cups)
2 tablespoons hot water

1 egg white
   flavoring (optional)

Place the sugar, water and egg white in a heatproof mixing bowl. Set the bowl over a saucepan half-filled with hot water and set the saucepan over low heat. Beat the mixture with a wooden spoon until it is smooth and glossy and will coat the back of the spoon. Add flavoring if desired. Remove pan from heat and the bowl from the pan. Spread lukewarm frosting on cake. It will set on cooling.

Mandarin Flan

6 portions

½ cup sifted all-purpose flour
2 large eggs
¼ cup superfine granulated
   sugar
6 tablespoons unsalted butter
¼ cup confectioners' sugar

1 large egg yolk
1 tablespoon orange-flavored
   liqueur
1 can (11 ounces) mandarin
   oranges
2 tablespoons apricot jam

Preheat oven to 350°F and position the shelf in the center. Oil an 8-inch sponge flan pan or layer-cake pan and line the base with wax paper. Oil the paper. Half-fill a saucepan with water, bring to a boil, then remove from heat. Sift the flour twice and set aside.

Place the eggs in a mixing bowl and whisk together lightly, using a balloon whisk, rotary beater or electric mixer. Beat in the sugar. Set the bowl over the pan of hot water; it should sit comfortably without touching the water. Whisk eggs and superfine sugar together until pale, thick and foamy. When fully whisked, the batter should hold the trail of the whisk for 3 seconds. Remove bowl from the pan and continue whisking for about 5 minutes, until the mixture is cool. Add flour gradually and lightly fold it in. Quickly turn the mixture into the prepared pan and bake for 25 to 30 minutes.

Remove the baked spongecake from the oven and stand the pan on a damp cloth for 30 seconds. Turn cake out on a wire rack and leave until completely cold.

Prepare the butter cream: Place the butter in a bowl and beat until creamy. Sieve the confectioners' sugar and add to the butter. Beat the egg yolk lightly. Add egg yolk and liqueur to the butter and beat together until smooth. Spread this butter cream evenly in the cold flan base or on top of the layer. Drain the orange segments and pat dry on paper towels. Arrange orange segments decoratively over the butter cream, closely overlapping. Warm the jam with 1 tablespoon water, sieve it, and brush it over the fruit to glaze it.

Variations: For pineapple spongecake flan, use well-drained canned pineapple pieces instead of orange segments. Flavor the butter cream with kirsch instead of orange liqueur. Glaze as for peach.

For raspberry spongecake flan, use fresh raspberries, flavor the butter cream with framboise liqueur, and glaze the fruit with red-currant jelly. Pipe on a border of whipped cream.

Bublanina

(Czechoslovakian Spongecake with Cherries)

6 to 8 portions

1 teaspoon butter	2 teaspoons lemon juice
4 eggs, separated	$\frac{1}{2}$ teaspoon vanilla extract
$\frac{5}{8}$ cup superfine granulated sugar	1 cup sifted self-rising flour
grated rind of 1 small lemon	1 cup canned pitted dark sweet cherries, drained

Preheat oven to 350°F. Coat a 9-inch layer-cake pan with the butter. In a large mixing bowl beat the egg yolks with a wire whisk, rotary beater or electric mixer until they are pale yellow. Beat in the sugar, lemon rind, lemon juice and vanilla. With a rubber scraper, lightly fold in the flour. In a separate mixing bowl beat the egg whites with a wire whisk or electric mixer until they stand in stiff peaks. With a metal spoon, lightly fold the beaten egg whites into the egg-yolk mixture. Fold in the drained cherries.

Pour the batter into the buttered cake pan and place it in the center of the oven. Bake for 45 to 50 minutes, until the top is golden brown and a skewer inserted into the cake comes out clean. Take the cake from the oven and leave it to cool on a wire rack before removing it from the pan.

Jam Spongecake

6 to 8 portions

3 medium-size eggs
½ cup superfine granulated sugar
¾ cup sifted all-purpose flour
1 tablespoon cornstarch
6 tablespoons melted clarified butter

few drops of vanilla extract
1 cup Vanilla Butter Cream (see Index)
¼ cup strawberry jam
confectioners' sugar

Preheat oven to 375°F. Make the cake, following the directions for Génoise (see Index). Pour the cake mixture into an 8-inch layer-cake pan. Bake for 25 to 30 minutes, until well risen and golden brown. Let the cake cool in the pan for 3 minutes, then invert on a wire rack to cool completely.

While the cake is cooling, make the butter cream and chill it. Cut the cake into 2 horizontal layers and spread the butter cream over the bottom layer. Spread the strawberry jam on the cut side of the top layer and sandwich the 2 layers together. Sift a little confectioners' sugar on the top of the cake before serving.

Variations: Sandwich the cake together with orange-flavored butter cream, then cover top and sides with more of the same butter cream. Decorate the outer top edge with candied orange slices.

Melt 2 ounces (2 squares) semisweet chocolate and spread in a thin layer on a sheet of wax paper. When the chocolate is set, use a 1-inch round cookie cutter to cut out circles of chocolate. Fill and cover a spongecake with Chocolate Butter Cream (see Index). Arrange the chocolate circles overlapping in lines across the top of the cake. Each line should overlap in the opposite direction to those on either side. Sift confectioners' sugar lightly over the top of the cake.

Sandwich a cake together with whipped cream lightly flavored with a fruit liqueur. Place slices of fresh or canned peaches on the cream before putting the layers together. Spread the top of the cake with more cream and arrange peach slices radiating around the center of the cake. Brush fruit with sieved raspberry jam, then sprinkle the center of the cake with a few chopped pistachios.

Jellied Spongecakes

24 cakes

7 tablespoons butter, melted
6 tablespoons superfine granulated sugar
3 eggs
¾ cup sifted all-purpose flour
⅛ teaspoon vanilla extract

Topping

1 envelope unflavored gelatin
¼ cup lemon juice
1⅞ cups orange juice
6 tablespoons heavy cream
1 can (11 ounces) mandarin oranges
2 bananas

Preheat oven to 425°F. Use 1 tablespoon of the butter to coat 2 baking pans, 8 × 12 inches. Put sugar and eggs in a bowl set in a pan half-filled with barely simmering water. Set the pan over low heat. Use a wire whisk, rotary beater or electric mixer to beat sugar and eggs together until the mixture forms a ribbon when the beater is lifted. Gradually beat in remaining butter. Remove pan from heat and lift bowl out of pan. With a wooden spoon, fold in the flour and vanilla and blend the mixture thoroughly.

Turn the batter into one of the prepared baking pans and smooth the top with a flat-bladed knife. Place the pan in the center of the oven and bake for 10 to 15 minutes, until the center of the cake springs back when lightly pressed with a fingertip. Remove pan from oven and let the cake cool slightly before turning it out on a wire rack to cool completely.

Meanwhile make the topping. Soften the gelatin in the lemon juice in a saucepan. Add orange juice and stir over low heat until gelatin is dissolved. Pour the mixture into the other baking pan and refrigerate until set. When it is completely firm, run a knife around the edge of the pan to loosen the sides. Quickly dip the bottom of the pan into hot water and invert the gelatin on the cake.

Whip the cream until stiff. Drain the oranges. Peel bananas and cut into thin slices. Spoon the whipped cream into a pastry bag fitted with a star tip. Arrange a row of mandarin orange segments across the top of the gelatin and place a row of banana slices next to it. Pipe a line of cream rosettes for the next row, and continue in the same order until all the fruit and cream have been used and the top of the gelatin is covered.

Cut the cake into squares and arrange them on a serving dish. Serve immediately.

Peach Spongecake

8 to 10 portions

¾ cup all-purpose flour
3 large eggs
6 tablespoons superfine
    granulated sugar

1 can (16 ounces) sliced peaches
1 cup heavy cream
½ to ¾ cup sliced almonds,
    toasted

Preheat oven to 350°F and position the shelf in the center. Brush a deep 6-inch round cake pan with oil or vegetable shortening. Line pan fully with wax paper and brush the paper with oil or shortening. Sprinkle with flour; shake the pan and tip out excess flour. Half-fill a saucepan with water, bring to a boil, then remove from heat. Sift the flour twice.

Place eggs in a mixing bowl and whisk lightly or beat with rotary beater or electric mixer. Add the sugar. Set the bowl over the pan of hot water and whisk eggs and sugar together until pale, thick and foamy. When fully whisked, the mixture should hold the trail of the whisk for 3 seconds. Remove bowl from the hot water and continue whisking for about 5 minutes, until the mixture is cool.

Add a quarter of the sifted flour and lightly fold it in. Repeat with remaining flour. When the flour is incorporated, lightly fold in 1 tablespoon warm water. Quickly turn the batter into the prepared pan and bake for 25 minutes. Reduce oven temperature to 325°F and bake for 40 minutes longer, until the surface of the cake feels firm in the center. Remove cake pan from the oven and stand it on a damp cloth towel for 30 seconds. Turn out the cake on a wire rack and leave until completely cold.

Drain the peach slices and pat dry on paper towels. Reserve a few of the best slices for decoration; chop the remainder. Whip the cream until thick. Slice the cold cake horizontally into 3 even layers. Spread the bottom layer with approximately 3 tablespoons of the whipped cream, then sprinkle with half of the chopped peaches. Place the center cake layer on top and spread with another 3 tablespoons of the whipped cream. Sprinkle with remaining chopped peaches. Top with the final cake layer. Coat the top and sides of the cake with all but 3 tablespoons of the cream. With a spatula, press the almonds, a few at a time, around the sides of the cake. Put remaining cream in a pastry bag fitted with a star tip and pipe stars of cream around the top outer edge of the cake. Decorate with reserved peach slices.

Variations: For strawberry spongecake, use rinsed and hulled fresh strawberries in place of canned peaches.

For lemon spongecake, add ½ teaspoon grated lemon rind to the whisked egg and sugar. Omit peaches, cream and almonds. Sandwich the layers together with Lemon Curd (see Volume 4 Index). Glaze with lemon-flavored Confectioners' Sugar Glaze (see Index) and decorate with candied lemon rind.

Madeleines

12 cakes

2 medium-size eggs
¼ cup superfine granulated
   sugar

½ cup sifted all-purpose flour
¼ cup melted clarified butter
   confectioners' sugar

Preheat oven to 375°F. Make the cake mixture following the directions for Génoise (see Index). Divide the mixture among the 12 depressions in a madeleine pan. Bake for 10 minutes, until well risen and golden brown. Let the cakes cool in the pan for 2 minutes, then invert them on a wire rack to cool completely. Sprinkle cakes with sieved confectioners' sugar and place on a serving plate.

Variations: Omit confectioners' sugar and instead dip the narrow end of each cake into melted chocolate, then quickly into toasted chopped nuts. Place cakes on a wire rack until the chocolate is firm.

Carefully split the cakes horizontally and sandwich together with whipped cream and sliced strawberries. Or split the cakes and spread the bottom portion with strawberry preserves and the tops with Vanilla Butter Cream (see Index). Sandwich the cakes together and sprinkle with confectioners' sugar.

Brush the top of each cake with sieved apricot jam and carefully dip into toasted shredded coconut.

Vanilla Butter Cream

about 1 cup

3 egg yolks
½ cup confectioners' sugar
   pinch of salt

6 ounces unsalted butter,
   softened
1½ teaspoons vanilla extract

Beat egg yolks, sugar and salt together with a whisk, rotary beater or electric mixer until the eggs form a ribbon when the beater is lifted. Beat in half of the softened butter, then the vanilla. Beat in the rest of the butter, bit by bit. Chill butter cream until it reaches the right texture for spreading. Then use at once, or refrigerate for up to three days.

Chocolate Ice-Cream Roll

8 portions

⅔ cup sifted all-purpose flour
   small pinch of salt
2 tablespoons powdered cocoa
3 large eggs

6 tablespoons superfine
   granulated sugar
1½ cups softened vanilla ice
   cream

Preheat oven to 400°F. Position the shelf just above the center. Prepare a jelly-roll pan, 13 × 9 inches, as described in Lining a Jelly-Roll Pan (see Index). Half-fill a large saucepan with water, bring to a boil, then remove from heat. Meanwhile, sift the flour twice, together with the salt and powdered cocoa.

Place the eggs in a mixing bowl and whisk lightly, using a balloon whisk, rotary beater or hand-held electric mixer. Add the sugar to the eggs. Set the mixing bowl over the pan of hot water. Whisk eggs and sugar together until the mixture is thick and foamy and will hold the trace of the whisk for 3 seconds. Remove the bowl from the heat and continue whisking for about 5 minutes, or until the mixture is cool. Fold in the flour gradually.

Quickly pour the batter into the prepared pan. Tilt the pan to spread the batter evenly in the corners. Bake for 8 to 10 minutes.

Meanwhile, prepare the equipment for turning out and rolling. Remove the baked spongecake from the oven and turn out immediately on the sugared paper. Peel off the lining paper, then trim off crisp edges. Mark 1 inch from the short edge nearest you with the back of a knife, then roll up firmly with the sugared paper inside. Hold in position for a few minutes, then transfer to a wire rack and leave until completely cold.

Unroll the cold roll carefully. Spread with ice cream to ¼ inch from the edges. Carefully roll up again, this time with the aid of the paper. Remove the paper, and place the roll seam side down on a plate. Sprinkle with superfine sugar. Freeze until ready to serve.

Variations: For vanilla and walnut roll, omit cocoa and increase the flour to ¾ cup. Sprinkle ⅓ cup finely chopped walnuts over the ice cream before rerolling.

For chocolate and coffee log, omit the ice cream. Make coffee butter icing with 6 tablespoons butter, 1½ cups confectioners' sugar and 2 teaspoons instant coffee powder dissolved in 2 tablespoons hot water. Use a quarter of the butter icing to fill the cold roll. Reroll the cake and ice it with remaining icing. Chill to make the icing firm.

For a traditional jelly roll, omit the cocoa and increase the flour to ¾ cup. Spread the turned-out and trimmed cake with ½ cup warm jam. Roll up, cool, and sprinkle with superfine sugar.

For chocolate and walnut roll, omit the ice cream. Make ½ cup vanilla-flavored Butter Icing (see Volume 1 Index) and beat in ⅓ cup chopped walnuts. Use this to fill the cold roll.

For honey spice sponge roll, omit cocoa and increase flour to ¾ cup. Sift 1½ teaspoons ground allspice with the flour and fold in 1 tablespoon hot water after the flour. Omit the ice cream and fill the cold roll with honey filling. Cream 4 ounces butter until very soft; gradually beat in 4 tablespoons honey. When thoroughly blended, add 1 tablespoon water and beat until very smooth.

For Christmas log, make a chocolate jelly roll and fill it with Vanilla Butter Cream (see Index). Cover with Chocolate Butter Frosting (see Volume 1 Index), swirled and marked with a fork to resemble the bark of a tree.

Biscuit Fin au Beurre

one 8-inch cake, 6 portions

4 tablespoons unsalted butter
¾ cup sifted all-purpose flour
1 tablespoon cornstarch

4 medium-size eggs
9 tablespoons superfine
   granulated sugar
   pinch of salt

Preheat oven to 375°F. Prepare an 8-inch layer-cake pan by buttering it, then sifting flour over it. Tap out excess flour. Dice the butter and place in a small bowl over a pan of hot water, until melted. Remove from heat. Clarify the butter. Sift together the flour and cornstarch.

Separate the eggs. Put the yolks and sugar into a warm bowl and whisk until thick. Whisk the egg whites with a pinch of salt until they form soft peaks. Add a big spoonful of egg white to the yolks, sift in a little of the flour mixture, and fold both in. Continue folding in egg white and flour mixture until all are used.

Quickly add the butter, a little at a time, and fold it in. Pour the batter into the prepared pan. Bake the cake for 25 to 30 minutes.

Célestines

18 petits fours

4 ounces Sweet Tart Pastry
(see Volume 2 Index)
1 recipe Biscuit Fin au Beurre
(see Index)
6 tablespoons apricot jam

1 cup confectioners' sugar
juice of 1 orange
⅓ cup chopped candied orange
peel

Preheat oven to 375°F. Roll out the pastry and use it to line 18 barquette molds or small round molds. Put a little apricot jam in the bottom of each mold. Fill them with the cake batter and smooth the tops. Bake in the center of the oven for 25 minutes, until the cake is firm and well risen. Turn cakes out on a wire rack and cool.

Melt remaining apricot jam in a small heavy pan over low heat and sieve it to make a glaze. Sift the confectioners' sugar into a heavy pan. Add the orange juice and 1 tablespoon cold water. Stir the mixture over low heat until the liquid is completely mixed with the sugar and the glaze is smooth and glossy. Remove from heat. Brush the top of each little cake with apricot jam. Cover with orange glaze and sprinkle with candied orange peel.

Variation: For *mirlitons,* line tartlet pans with sweet tart pastry, as for Célestines. Make the *biscuit fin au beurre.* Crush about 5 macaroons and fold into the batter. Put a little apricot purée in the base of each tartlet and top with the cake batter. Decorate each one with 3 split almonds in the shape of a trefoil. Bake like Célestines, reducing the baking time to about 20 minutes. Sprinkle with confectioners' sugar before serving.

Dobos Torte

Created by Joseph Dobos, famous 19th century Hungarian gourmet.

8 to 10 portions

Chocolate Butter Cream with Sugar Syrup

4 ounces (4 squares)
semisweet cooking
chocolate
8 ounces unsalted butter
1 teaspoon vanilla extract
1 cup granulated sugar
¼ cup water
6 egg yolks

Dobos Spongecake

2 tablespoons unsalted butter,
softened
1 cup plus 2 tablespoons
sifted all-purpose flour
6 eggs, separated
½ cup superfine granulated sugar
1 teaspoon vanilla extract

Caramel Glaze

1 cup confectioners' sugar

First make the butter cream: Melt the chocolate in a small saucepan over low heat, stirring occasionally. As soon as chocolate is melted, remove pan from heat and set it aside. In a mixing bowl cream the butter and vanilla together until light and fluffy. Set aside. Mix the sugar and water in a small heavy saucepan and stir over low heat until sugar dissolves. Increase heat to moderately high and bring the syrup to a boil. Cover the pan and boil gently for 5 minutes. Uncover the pan and continue boiling the syrup until it reaches 230° to 234°F on a candy thermometer, or until it will form a short thread when a little is lifted out with a fork. Remove pan from heat and set the syrup aside to cool slightly.

Meanwhile, in another mixing bowl beat the egg yolks with a wire whisk, rotary beater or electric mixer until thick and pale yellow in color. Beating constantly, pour the hot syrup into the egg yolks in a thin stream. (A whisk or hand-held electric mixer is the best tool to use for this step.) Do this mixing gradually so the eggs do not scramble. Beat the mixture vigorously until it is very thick and completely cold. Gradually beat the cooled syrup into the creamed butter. Slowly stir in the melted chocolate. Leave the butter cream at room temperature while baking the spongecake.

Preheat oven to 350°F. Coat a shallow 8-inch round baking pan with 1 teaspoon of the softened butter. Sprinkle in 1 teaspoon of the flour and tip and rotate the pan to distribute the flour evenly. Shake out any excess flour. Set the pan aside.

Make the Dobos spongecake layers. In a mixing bowl beat the egg yolks and half of the sugar with a wire whisk, rotary beater or electric mixer until mixture is thick and pale yellow. Add vanilla and set the bowl to one side. In another mixing bowl beat the egg whites until frothy. Add remaining sugar to whites and beat until they are stiff. Gently fold the egg whites into the egg-yolk mixture. Sift 1 cup of the flour, a little at a time, into the egg mixture, folding it in gently until just incorporated.

Spoon one sixth of the batter into the prepared pan, enough to make a layer about ¼ inch thick. Place the pan in the center of the oven and bake the cake layer for about 15 minutes, until it is lightly browned. Remove pan from oven, run a knife around the inside of the rim, and reverse the layer on a wire rack. Set it aside to cool.

Butter and flour the pan again with another teaspoon each of butter and flour and spoon in another one sixth of the batter. Bake the other layers in the same way as the first until all 6 layers have been baked.

If you have more than 1 cake pan and your oven is large enough, you can bake 2 or more layers at the same time.

For the top of the cake, select the layer with the best surface. Place it on a shallow baking sheet or a sheet of foil. Lightly oil the area around the cake so the caramel will not stick to the pan when it is poured on the cake. With the blunt side of a knife, make 8 to 10 wedge-shaped indentations on the layer, but do not cut through the layer.

Make the caramel: Melt the confectioners' sugar in a small heavy saucepan over low heat, stirring constantly. Cook the sugar until it is smooth and golden brown, pressing out any lumps with the back of the spoon. Remove pan from heat and quickly pour the caramel over the marked sponge layer. With an oiled knife, smooth the caramel evenly over the surface. With the blunt side of the oiled knife, make wedge-shaped indentations over the previous ones, cutting the wedges nearly through to the cake. Let the caramel harden. Refrigerate the chocolate butter cream until it reaches the right spreading consistency.

To assemble the cake, place one of the remaining 5 layers on a plate. Spread the layer with approximately one sixth of the chocolate butter cream. Place another layer on top and spread with another one sixth of the butter cream. Continue in this manner, making alternate layers of cake and butter cream, ending with the caramel-glazed top layer. Leave a little of the remaining butter cream for decoration and spread the rest on the sides of the cake. Place the butter cream for decoration in a pastry bag fitted with a star tip and pipe it around the top and bottom edges. Chill cake until butter cream is firm. Cut into portions, following the indentations on the top, using a hot knife.

Part Five

A CHILDREN'S BIRTHDAY PARTY

Although there are adults who claim to be ambivalent about celebrating their birthdays, it is a rare child indeed who does not feel that his or her own birthday is the most important of all holidays and that a birthday party is the only proper way to celebrate this very special day. For the adults who face the challenge of producing this event some careful planning and the observation of a few guidelines will reduce the stress and mayhem that sometimes seem inevitable when entertaining groups of children.

This cheerful menu is designed to appeal to children who are over 6 years old and who are not yet in their teens. A much quoted rule of thumb is to limit the number of guests to the number of years being celebrated, thus this menu is planned to serve 8 to 10 children, but it can easily be adjusted up or down.

Children's birthday parties seem to work best when they take place as early as possible in the day and last a maximum of an activity-packed 3 hours. This party menu works extremely well as a lunch on Saturday or Sunday, although it can as easily take place on a weekday, after school. In such an event you may decided to narrow the menu down a bit and concentrate on the fruit platter and desserts.

Everything except the Sloppy Joes can and should be prepared ahead. Both cakes may be baked the day before, although the fresh raspberry cake is better assembled on the morning of the party. The fresh fruit for the Tutti-Frutti Platter can be cut up several hours ahead and refrigerated. The platter looks most attractive if as many different kinds of fruits as possible are included, making for a colorful and varied arrangement.

The Sloppy Joe sandwiches are pure kid food, simple and satisfying and as far away from anything gourmet as you can get. Children tend to be extremely conservative in their tastes, so avoid any temptation to jazz things up with fancy spices or exotic ingredients. Remember, this party is for them, so keep it simple. You may want to consider cooking the beef in an electric skillet at a buffet table if you are holding the party in a recreation room or other childproof area. Don't hesitate to dress yourself up in a chef's costume or as a short-order cook—children appreciate any amount of corny humor.

There are two birthday cakes, as is only right to make this important occasion even more festive. The two cakes not only look pretty together, but taste good together, too, so everyone can have a little bit of each. Fresh lemonade goes well throughout the meal, but don't forget to have a lot of milk on hand as well.

Keep decorations colorful, simple and inexpensive—balloons, crepe paper ribbons, and plastic or paper plates and cups are standard and expected party fare. Get lots of little party favors, some good old standard games like Pin the Tail, a pack of crayons for each child, and the biggest roll of plain brown paper you can find. Then let 'em rip, relax, remember your own birthday parties, and have fun.

MARKET LIST

Meat

ground beef (2 pounds)

Fruits and Vegetables

For Tutti-Frutti Platter, select from a minimum of 3 or 4 of the following categories according to what is available:

apples (2 red, 2 yellow)
bananas (2)
apricots (4 to 6)
cherries (1 pound)
seedless grapes (1 pound, green or purple or some of each)
melon (1 small, not watermelon)

oranges (2 to 3)
peaches (2 to 3)
pears (2 to 3)
plums (4 to 6)
strawberries (1 pint)
tangerines (3 to 4)
fresh mint (1 bunch) optional

onion (1 medium)
green pepper (1 medium)
celery
lettuce (1 iceberg)
raspberries or strawberries (2 pints)
lemons (10 to 12)

Staples

cream cheese (8 ounces)
sugar
vanilla extract
milk (2 cups for cooking, plus enough to serve as beverage)
heavy whipping cream (1 pint)
unsalted butter (1 pound)

ketchup
salt
hamburger or frankfurter buns (8 to 10)
Cheddar cheese (½ pound)
potato chips
eggs (6)
unsweetened powdered cocoa
cake flour

all-purpose flour
baking soda
double-acting baking powder
unsweetened chocolate (2 ounces)
confectioners' sugar (1 pound)
raspberry jam

Other

party favors
balloons
paper or plastic plates
paper cups or plastic glasses

plastic spoons and forks
paper napkins
party games
jelly beans

brown paper (several big rolls)
crayons
birthday candles

A CHILDREN'S BIRTHDAY PARTY LUNCH FOR 8 TO 10 CHILDREN

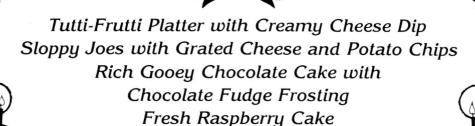

Tutti-Frutti Platter with Creamy Cheese Dip
Sloppy Joes with Grated Cheese and Potato Chips
Rich Gooey Chocolate Cake with
Chocolate Fudge Frosting
Fresh Raspberry Cake
Beverage Suggestions:
Real Homemade Lemonade, Milk

Real Homemade Lemonade

16 to 20 portions

4 cups water
2 cups sugar
1½ cups lemon juice (8 to 10 lemons)

3 quarts cold water
lemon slices for garnish

Heat 4 cups water and sugar in a saucepan until sugar is completely dissolved. Remove from heat and pour syrup into a large pitcher. Stir in lemon juice and cold water. Float lemon slices on top. Refrigerate until serving time. Serve in the pitcher or a pretty punch bowl.

Tutti-Frutti Platter

Select the ripest, prettiest fruits, choosing according to what is in season and available in the market. Try to include at least 3 or 4 different types of fruit. The amounts indicated are approximate, depending on how great a variety you are able to include.

Choose from:

2 red-skinned apples, such as McIntosh
2 yellow-skinned apples, such as Golden Delicious
2 bananas
4 to 6 ripe apricots
1 pound Bing cherries
1 pound seedless grapes, green or purple, or some of each

1 small ripe melon, any variety except watermelon
2 to 3 oranges
2 to 3 peaches
2 to 3 ripe pears
4 to 6 plums
1 pint strawberries
3 to 4 tangerines
1 lemon, for juice
1 bunch fresh mint, for garnish

Prepare fruit as follows: Wash, quarter and core apples but do not peel. Cut each quarter in half, and sprinkle with lemon juice. Peel bananas and cut into bite-size chunks. Sprinkle with lemon juice. Wash and dry apricots. Cut each in half and remove pit. Sprinkle cut surface with lemon juice. Wash and dry cherries but leave the stems, as they make perfect handles. Wash and dry grapes and cut into small clusters. Cut melon in half lengthwise and remove seeds. Slice into thin wedges or spears and cut away the skin. Sprinkle with lemon juice. Peel oranges and separate into sections. Wash and dry

peaches. Cut in half and remove the pit. Cut into bite-size wedges. Wash, quarter and core the pears. Cut into wedges and sprinkle with lemon juice. Wash and dry plums. Cut in half and remove the pit and cut into wedges if they are large. Wash strawberries and dry on paper towels. Cut them in half if they are large, otherwise leave them whole and unhulled. Peel tangerines and separate into sections.

Arrange fruit attractively on a large platter. Garnish with fresh mint and refrigerate until serving time. Serve with a bowl of creamy cheese dip.

Creamy Cheese Dip

makes about 2 cups

8 ounces cream cheese
4 tablespoons sugar
½ teaspoon vanilla extract (optional)

½ cup milk
½ cup heavy cream

Blend cream cheese with sugar and vanilla. Beat in milk with wooden spoon until mixture is smooth. Beat heavy cream until stiff and fold into cream cheese mixture. Refrigerate until serving time.

Sloppy Joes

8 to 10 portions

2 tablespoons butter
2 pounds ground beef
1 medium-size onion, finely chopped
1 medium-size green pepper, cored, seeded and finely chopped
2 celery ribs, finely chopped
½ cup ketchup

1 cup water
salt
2 cups finely shredded lettuce
8 to 10 hamburger or frankfurter buns, lightly toasted
2 cups shredded Cheddar cheese

Melt the butter in a large skillet and brown the beef, stirring frequently with a large fork or wooden spoon. Add onion, pepper and celery and cook, stirring, for 5 minutes, until vegetables have wilted. Add ketchup and water and simmer uncovered for 15 minutes, stirring frequently. Taste for seasoning when mixture is ready to serve and add salt to taste.

Place a small handful of shredded lettuce on each bun and spoon ground beef on top of it. Pass a bowl of grated cheese and additional shredded lettuce for individual toppings.

Serve with potato chips.

Fresh Raspberry Cake

One 9-inch cake

½ cup sugar
3 large eggs, at room temperature
1 tablespoon vanilla extract
½ cup sifted all-purpose flour
a pinch of salt

4 tablespoons unsalted butter, melted and cooled
1 cup heavy cream
2 tablespoons granulated sugar
2 pints raspberries
1 cup raspberry jam

Preheat oven to 350°F. Line two 9-inch cake pans with rounds of buttered and floured wax paper.

Beat sugar and eggs together in a large bowl until mixture turns creamy white. Add vanilla and beat at high speed until eggs have doubled in volume. Gently fold in flour and salt, deflating the egg mass as little as possible. When the flour has been incorporated, fold in the melted butter, a little at a time. Pour batter into prepared cake pans and bake 20 minutes, or until sides of cake have receded slightly from the pan. Top of cake should be golden in color and springy to the touch. Let cool in pans for 5 to 10 minutes, then remove to a cake rack and peel away wax paper.

While cake is cooling, whip the heavy cream together with the sugar until it is thick and billowy. Pick over raspberries and discard any that are blemished.

Spread a layer of raspberry jam on one of the cake layers. Top with a layer of fresh raspberries and one-third of the whipped cream. Put second cake layer over, and spread a layer of jam on top. Spread top and sides of cake with whipped cream, then decorate top with fresh raspberries. Refrigerate cake until serving time.

Variation: This cake can also be made with strawberries. Substitute strawberry jam for raspberry and sieve before using.

Rich Gooey Chocolate Layer Cake

This cake may be baked the day before the party. Use the same recipe to make cupcakes if you prefer. Spoon batter into lined muffin tins and bake 20 minutes.

one 9-inch cake or 24 cupcakes

4 ounces unsalted butter, at room temperature
1¾ cups granulated sugar
3 eggs
1¼ cups milk
1 teaspoon vanilla extract

1 cup unsweetened powdered cocoa
1 teaspoon salt
2 cups cake flour
1¼ teaspoons baking soda
½ teaspoon double-acting baking powder

Preheat oven to 350°F. Butter and flour two 9-inch round cake pans. Measure all ingredients into a large bowl and beat with an electric mixer at low speed, scraping sides of bowl with a spatula, until batter is well mixed. Continue beating mixture at high speed for 5 minutes. Pour equal amounts of batter into prepared cake pans and bake for 30 to 35 minutes. Place cake pans on wire racks for 15 to 20 minutes to cool. Remove cake from pans and cool completely before frosting.

Chocolate Fudge Frosting

enough to fill and frost a 2-layer cake or 24 cupcakes

½ cup heavy cream
2 ounces (2 squares) unsweetened chocolate
4 cups confectioners' sugar

4 ounces unsalted butter, at room temperature
1 teaspoon vanilla extract

Place cream and chocolate in top of double boiler over hot water and stir until the chocolate is melted. Beat in sugar until completely blended; remove from heat. Cut butter into pieces and add with vanilla. Stir until smooth.

INDEX